From Boo, With Love

Unpublished Stories and Verse

From Boo, With Love

Unpublished Stories and Verse

Richard W. Turner, Sr.

COROIN BOOKS

Copyright © 2026 by Richard W. Turner, Sr.

All rights reserved. No part of this publication may be reproduced, stored in a retrieval system, or transmitted in any form or by any means, including electronic, mechanical, photocopying, recording, or otherwise, without the prior written permission of the publisher, except in the case of brief quotations embodied in critical reviews and certain other noncommercial uses permitted by U.S. copyright law.

For permission requests, contact books@coroin.com

Published by Coroin Books
https://coroin.com/books

ISBNs
eBook (EPUB): 978-1-963770-15-5
Paperback: 978-1-963770-16-2
Hardcover: 978-1-963770-17-9
LCCN (Library of Congress Control Number): 2025927670

Cover illustration by Carlos Maraver
https://vectorlance.com

Every effort has been made by the author and publisher to ensure that the information in this book is accurate at the time of publication. Neither the author nor the publisher shall be held liable for any loss, damage, or disruption caused by errors or omissions, whether such errors result from negligence, accident, or any other cause. Readers are encouraged to verify any information before taking action.

Foreword

ASHLIN S. LARSON

Allow me to first start by saying thank you. Thank you for being a part of this, and for whatever circumstances brought you here today.

It was just a few short months ago that my Dad asked me to help him continue my Great-Grandfather's legacy by re-releasing his books. *Third Chance, Revelation —At Last, Stories From The Hump*, and now: *From Boo, With Love*. And what a journey it's been! Countless hours, questions and suggestions, and many, many meetings, just to bring this book to you, Dearest Reader.

On a personal level, reading these four books has been both heartwarming and informative, and yet a little bittersweet. As I took on the editorial role that many women in my family have shared the responsibilities of over the decades, it's safe to say that I was impacted. Reading and (lightly) editing the honest words and memories of a man, as well as hearing his daughter's tone and persuasion for grammar in the way that things were edited throughout these books, has been immeasurably valuable to me. My Gramma, who had a Master's degree in Library Sciences, passed at the beginning of last year. And if you know my family, or knew Sharyn, you can understand just how much of a loss it has been for us. She was beloved. Similar to how my Great-Grandmother was beloved by my Great-Grandfather, as he so eloquently detailed in his second book, *Revelation—At Last.*

> "We all feel this hurtful loss;
> Let memories come to you." -Boo

He was affectionately dubbed 'Boo,' and you can read about how he earned that nickname towards the end of this book. Last year, while I was reading through his catalog of content for the first time, it became abundantly clear that Boo had an incredible sense of humor. I found myself laughing, crying from laughter, just plain crying, and adding so so many commas while wishing that I could've known him. I have so many questions. Unfortunately, reading his books is the closest I'll get since Boo passed mere months after my 1st birthday.

Most of Boo's words were written from a posture of grief and memory, and through his pain, he humbly demonstrated what was most important to him: Jesus Christ and his family. His passion and the depths of his love for the Lord and his sweetheart, Caroline, are a testament to his life, as well as the way he served his community and his country, as both a Boy Scout of America (member and executive) and as a World War II veteran.

A few more scouting stories you'll get, alas, you'll find no war stories in these pages. Those were collected in his third book, *Stories from the Hump.* Boo's fourth and final book contains a selection of stories and poems that have not been previously published, which is divided into two parts: **Stories** and **Verse**. The Stories are presented in historical order, following the author's life. The Verses are presented in chronological order when written. The subtitle for each chapter includes the date it was written, if known.

I am a continuation of this legacy of great love that my great-grandparents shared. By proxy, YOU, Dearest Reader, are also a part of this legacy. By reading this book, you are honoring their love and memories.

I encourage you to share, honor, and respect others in whatever capacity makes sense for you. But, above all, and to quote Boo, "Love one another. ALWAYS."

Now, with another year beneath our belts and the wounds of our hearts working so dutifully to scab over, it is my joy and honor to present a book that four generations of my family have worked on. Grief has a funny way of bringing people together. If you aren't already considered as such, I hope these words will make you feel like part of the family, too. And, to those of you who knew Boo, I hope you find comfort in these pages and are reminded of the man you once knew, keeping his memory alive as you read. Remember that Richard, Dick, Boo, or whatever moniker you knew him by, isn't gone. He is more than content in Heaven, with his sweetheart and their "Sweet Jesus".

Almost a decade ago, my Gramma and Grandad gifted me a rhyming dictionary during my songwriting phase. I always kind of questioned this, as I am a product of my generation and the age of technology. But over the years, it's something I've turned to more times than I can count. While working on these books, I found out it was something she did for her dad (Boo), too. Thus, it is in their honor that I sign off with a poem. Also included is a Valentine's Day card from Boo II to Boo, dated 2002.

Another year has come and passed,
And again, I find myself reminiscing on the past.
Years ago, Boo wrote these books for you.
Now, the time has come to share them—at last!

They may make you cry,
They will surely make you laugh,
But most of all, I hope they remind you to
Think fondly of time that has passed.
Every smile and every laugh.

So, without further ado, please enjoy: *From Boo, With Love*.

Ashlin S. Larson
Galveston, Texas
February 14, 2026

> I had great plans
> ahead of time
> to get some cards
> with a pretty rhyme.
>
> But circumstances changed
> those plans of mine.
>
> But please, will you still
> be my VALENTINE?
>
> Love
>
> Love,
> Daddy
> (Boo II)

Contents

An Interesting Life   1

STORIES   7

1. The Turner Navy   9
2. Will Rogers And Wiley Post   13
3. Snow Camping   17
4. A Heel Of A Story   21
5. Bridge, Anyone?   25
6. Breaking Away   29
7. Art Development   33
8. Experiencing A Hurricane   37
9. VW "BUG" vs CADILLAC   41
10. Over The Fence   43
11. Burning Stick Coffee   47
12. A Trip To Philmont   51
13. Shipwrecked   57
14. Nudes vs Butterflys   61

15.	Turner Tuna Recipe	63
VERSE		65
16.	A Pain In The Back	67
17.	Flowers For Caroline	69
18.	Hippity Hip	71
19.	For Diane	73
20.	Chew On This One	75
21.	Son Canyon	77
22.	Advent Story 2002	79
23.	Boxes, Boxes, Boxes	81
24.	Thanksgiving 2002	83
25.	Memories	87
26.	Her Guiding Hand	91
27.	Who's Counting---I Am	93
28.	Favorite Words	95
29.	Clouds	97
30.	Lost In Heaven	99
31.	Boo Who?	103
32.	I Just Know	107
33.	Restaurant Relief	109
34.	My Hole-In-One	113
35.	Dreary Days?	117
36.	Lonesome Salesman	121
37.	Reunion	125
38.	Retirement!!?	127

39.	Oh, Bearded One	131
40.	Ring	135
41.	Four-Letter Words	137
42.	Turtles & Rabbits	139
43.	My Dear Friend Arthur Lynip	143
44.	What Is This Christmas Thing?	147
45.	Three Brothers	151
46.	Our Commitment	153
47.	Butterfly Angels	157
48.	The UTI Blues	161
49.	Carolines Gift	165
50.	My Son	167
51.	Seeking Sincerity	171
52.	Oh, Country 'Tis Of Thee---Ring	173
53.	What Is That Trophy	179
54.	Berod At Times	185
About		187
Also by		189

An Interesting Life

July 29, 2003

THE FOLLOWING MAY SEEM like a case of vanity or ego. Actually, I would like to sort of chronicle a life that has led me in many directions. There have been lots of failures, but I credit my Lord Jesus for having led me into more successes that have allowed me to express His talents through me.

*The most awesome and rewarding event of my life was meeting and marrying Caroline. We were married 56 ½ years when she was called to be with her Sweet Jesus on December 7, 2000.

We were blessed with three children: Sharyn, Rick (Richard Jr.), and Nancy. They and their spouses have presented eight grandchildren, three grandchildren-in-law, and so far four great-grandchildren and two step-grands.

All of this as a result of our six-week courtship during wartime in 1944. Not bad!!!

- Born March 14, 1924.

- I remember Charles Lindbergh flying the Atlantic Ocean in 1927.

- I remember the Great Depression and hearing of soup lines.

- Started Kindergarten in January 1929, not quite 5 years old.

- My parents took my two brothers and me to see the evangelist, Billy Sunday. I remember him as a dynamic speaker and his message of salvation. At the time, I did not understand it.

- I remember seeing a movie titled "Wings." It was a silent movie. "Talkies" had not yet arrived.

- At about age 10, I entered an art contest sponsored by Spaulding Bakeries. Won 2nd place- a huge box of watercolors. (Better than the 1st place red wagon, I had one!)

- I remember hearing about Will Rogers and aviator Willie Post going down and being lost somewhere in Alaska. I was mixing concrete for a brick mason that day.

- Had a small drawing published in a national publication, for an illustration of an article by one of my high school teachers.

- In high school, I had a small part in our Senior play. Later, a more important part — the villain — in another play called "And the lamp went out."

- Sang as a tenor in a double quartet and in the school chorus. Played a harmonica in a four-man (boy) harmonica "band."

- A member of the track team. I raced in the heel-and-toe competition.

- A contest was conducted in my high school for a permanent design of a graduation ring. My design was accepted and used for many years. I was awarded the first ring made, and I graduated that following January, 1942.

- Became an Eagle Scout in 1939. Eventually earned 51 Merit Badges and a double set of Bronze, Gold, and Silver Palms.

- Our hometown was a stopping-over place for the big bands and entertainers of that time, so I dated and danced to such bands as Benny Goodman, Glen Miller, Vaughn Monroe, the Andrews Sisters, Gene Krupa, and many others of the Big Band Era.

- Enlisted in the U.S. Army Air Corps, went through Primary, Basic, and Twin-engine Advanced Pilot training. Earned my Silver Wings as a Military Pilot. Because I was an Eagle Scout, they waived the two-year college requirement.

- Met and married the Love of my life, Caroline Elizabeth Davis.

- On our honeymoon, we went to New York City, where we saw Frank Sinatra perform live.

- Served overseas in the China, Burma, India Theater of War. Flew 72 ½ combat missions. Awarded the Distinguished Flying Cross, Air Medal with cluster, Presidential Unit Citation, Good Conduct Medal, Asiatic Medal with 3 battle stars, and other decorations.

- Returned to IBM after the war. As their copy artist, I worked on and did the artwork for the Terminal Leave Bond given to all veterans after WWII, as mustering-out pay. This was the only time negotiable paper that was printed outside of the mint. I did the art and photography for the making of the copper plates used in the printing process.

- Opened my own photo-engraving, lithographic offset plate, and commercial art business, with my brother-in-law Norman Davis. It was called the Commercial Photoengraving Co.

- Awarded the District Scouter Trophy, Scouter's Award, and the Scouter's Key as a Cubmaster and District Training Chairman for volunteer service.

- Became a Master Mason in 1946.

- Later earned the Order of the Arrow Ordeal and Brotherhood membership. Awarded the honorary Vigil membership.

- Completed the 10-year training program and received a Fellowship as a Professional Scouter.

- Painted and sold numerous oil paintings. Entered several art shows in southeastern states. One huge drawing hung in the Atlantic Coast Line Railroad Building in Washington, DC.

- Watched Apollo 11 take off from Cape Canaveral, which carried Neil Armstrong, the first human to walk on the moon. I was there to see the launch.

- Did many wood carvings and sculptures, including Church wall hangings and portable communion sets, and cabinetry for lawyers and doctors. At least 1,000 pieces.

- Served as a Deacon for one term and as an Elder for two terms in the Presbyterian Church.

- We were baptized in the Catawba River in 1974.

- Caroline and I took a hot-air balloon ride for over an hour and a half for my 70th birthday.

- I was presented with my 50-year Masonic pin in 1996.

- I was on the edge of heaven March 8, 1998, but God let me return to my Caroline.

- We climbed to the top of Massada, Israel, in 1999.

- We were baptized (re-dedicated) in the Jordan River in 1999.

- We took cruises to Alaska, the Caribbean Islands twice, Hawaii on our 50th Anniversary, and through the Panama Canal. We traveled to Europe, South America, the Middle East, Canada, and many of the United States.

- I have been on five continents, including Africa. Been to the Sahara Desert, the jungles of this country, Africa, South America, and India. Went through the Suez Canal and swam in the Bay of India, the Atlantic and Pacific Oceans, and the Caribbean Sea. Waded in the North Sea, the streams of Ireland, in the Catskill, Adirondack, Smoky, Ozark, and other mountains. I have even been in a stream in the Himalayan Mountains.

- I have flown over the Mississippi, Amazon, Nile, Congo, and Brahmaputra Rivers. Also over the Catskill, Smokey, Ozark, Adirondack, Rocky, Sierra, and Himalayan Mountains.

- Written four books of life stories and poems. Two poems were put to music and used as church anthems.

- Appeared on two television documentaries as a historical guest, a WWII pilot.

- Participated as MC for many appearances in schools, churches, and civic groups, telling the story and history of the CBI during WWII.

- Done black-and-white pen sketches of historical buildings.

- For over 12 years, designed and directed the construction of Vacation Bible School entertainment and instruction sets for children. Also, developed a fourteen-station Easter Drive-through and other sets for church programs.

- At age 79, I took up pen sketching of old run-down tobacco barns and farm barns.

Most everyone who has attained the age of eighty has many experiences to share with the present generation. Not all have been military pilots during a war, nor done many of the things listed above. But many have done things that I have not dreamed of doing, or seen, or lived through. I have been in two major floods, six hurricanes, seen and been in two tornadoes, but I am alive to tell about them. How blessed I am.

Do yourself a favor. Ask someone of age to tell you about his or her life. I can almost guarantee that you will not be bored.

I do not list these few events of my life to boast or try to impress anyone. I know who I am, where I have been, and what I have done. This information is a sharing of my and Caroline's lives together. To chronicle her life would be more impressive than mine because she chose to live and put up with me. I miss my Caroline, and feel I am only half a person because of losing her. But she is with the Lord, and until I am called to be with her again, this is my way of honoring her, by sharing what I can remember of an interesting life.

Bless her. I love her always.

STORIES

The Turner Navy

For a person who never particularly liked the water, except to drink and bathe in, I must tell you about our boat. It was not a ship; just a boat. Normally, a boat is a means of going from one place to another, over the water. However, the vessel that we had never took us anyplace---on land, sea, or air. Our Navy took us to more faith and trust in our ever-loving God. Let me explain.

When I was a small lad, our family did not go fishing like many others. We did the normal things like picnicking, some travel, had plenty of family outings, etc. But fishing was not our priority. Dad took us three brothers out on a pond or two, and we did learn how to bait a hook, cast a line, row a boat, and appreciate catching a small fish once in a while. But we never got "hooked" on fishing. We ate fish from the store. The biggest fish I ever caught as a child was a little sunfish—hardly big enough for two bites, after scaling. I got more mosquito bites than fish bites!

During my wait to come home from India after WWII ended, some of us went "fishing " in the Bay of India outside of Karachi. The dhow-style boat was picturesque, powered by a sail and an Indian crew of 3 or 4. The crew even had a charcoal brazier fired up to cook the fish we were supposed to catch. The only thing that was caught was a baby shark about 18 inches long. Even then, the Lord was watching over us home-bound pilots, because we had been swimming over the side of that dhow just minutes before. We were glad Mamma shark wasn't looking for her baby! Be patient, I'll get to the Turner Navy.

After the war, while living in Wilmington, NC, I did some pier and surf fishing. I even caught some Blues and other types of fish. It was fun, but not enough for me to want more than a rod and saltwater reel. Much less a BOAT!!

By now, you probably understand that I am not a sailor. Also, you probably understand that I am not a fisherman. Further, you probably understand the first sentence of this story better.

In 1959, I went to work for the Boy Scouts of America. My first assignment was in Anderson, SC. Leaving my wife Caroline and our children, Sharyn, Rick, and Nancy in Wilmington, I went ahead to establish myself in this new position. But first, I had to go to a six-week training course, while Caroline started packing up our earthly possessions for this move. We would move from the sea coast inland, to the foothills and mountains of western SC. A couple of lakes, but away from all that water.

When the family arrived, and we were all together again, one thing was mandatory: we had to eat. This meant trips to the grocery store. Caroline took care of buying food from the local supermarket. We had rented a house. The supermarket had one of those promotions where you registered for some sort of prize. She paid no attention to what was to be awarded, but she did register. Three times she registered.

One afternoon, a newly made neighbor across the street from us came over, all excited. The Turner family had won the drawing at the local supermarket!!! We were the new owners of-------a 15-foot fiberglass FISHING BOAT, an outboard engine, a trailer on which to haul it, and a gas can. The works!!! We had lived on the coast for 12 years, didn't especially like the activities regarding the water, and couldn't afford the price of a can of fuel to run this wonderful BOAT. I didn't even have a hitch on our car with which to haul it from the supermarket to our new home!!!

Whoopee!!!

About that time, one of the local Cubmasters arrived at our house to congratulate us on our good fortune. Lots of people seemed to have heard about this, except us. But then, we got no phone call because our phone had not been installed. The neighbor said an announcement had been made at the store, and the winner was to come claim the prize. So the Cubmaster friend said he would take us to the store to claim our BOAT and, because he had a trailer hitch on his station wagon, he would haul it to our new home. Now you know how we acquired the TURNER NAVY.

But what does this have to do with a trip of faith?

We had come into this new career, carrying some rather heavy financial burdens. One of our daughters had been hospitalized 23 times. Two trips to Duke Hospital for surgery, six weeks in Johns-Hopkins Hospital in Baltimore, just to name a few. Plus untold Doctors and medications. This will give you an idea of our situation. Just the everyday cost of raising a family added to our need for some relief.

The faith of Caroline was the true strength of this story. She never faltered in her trust that the Lord would get us through. That faith and trust got our daughter cared for and on the road to recovery. (Today she is 57 years old, a wife, mother, and grandmother.)

I am convinced that God provided the winning ticket so we could win a boat that we had no use for. Neither of us was a boat person. If we put that boat in the water and then tried to sell it, it would be a used boat. If we could sell this nice new outfit, it would go a long way towards paying some of those bills.

So we sold the *Turner Navy*. We used that boat to take us down a path of deeper trust in our Lord. Many times this story comes to mind, especially when times of financial, decision-making, or emotional stress come along. That BOAT carried us, landlubbers, over places no real boat ever could.

Praise the Lord for the *Turner Navy*.

WILL ROGERS AND WILEY POST

AUGUST 4, 2003

WILL ROGERS WAS BORN in 1879 as William Penn Adair Rogers in the Midwest before Oklahoma became a state. He became famous as an actor, humorist, and a country wit and statesman. He visited the President and appeared before Congress on occasion.

Willey Post was a famous aviator who set speed records and some endurance records in the early days of man's flight. He wore a patch over one eye, and he was often seen flying his special airplane, the "Winnic Mae." He flew over my hometown once in that beautiful white monoplane.

I remember these men because they occasionally appeared on the Paramount News screen when we went to the movies. (Black and white only.) There was no such thing as television then. Our news was received by radio, those movie newsreels, or by mouth. These men decided to make a flight around the world together in the "Winnie Mae."

This story is of a young boy, 11 years old. It takes place on a hot summer day in 1935.

My dad provided well for his family. He was well paid at $22 to $24 a week as a ladies' shoe designer and pattern maker. My mother was a stay-at-home mom, as were most mothers of that time. So what I was doing that day was not a necessity to provide for the family. I was mixing mortar for a bricklayer.

We kids in the neighborhood did the usual playing of sandlot baseball, mumbly-peg, cops and robbers, cowboys and Indians (we even were allowed to play with toy guns!), and other games of tag. We roller-skated and made orange crate scooters. Some even had bicycles, although I did not get my one-and-only 24" used bicycle until I was about 13.

Being a kid did not keep me from getting a job at the end of the street we lived on, with the men building a new house. Dad provided well, so pay was not the incentive. Pay? Zero. Zilch. No pay. We kids, did this kind of thing because it made us feel good to "work around adults." The workmen got free labor. We kids, got training and satisfaction. Not bad.

My job that day? Mixing mortar to hold the cinder blocks together (they are cement blocks today, but back then they used cinders, too, or so they told us), just as they do today. Except that the mortar was not brought to the building site by truck, or mixed in an on-site powered mixer. The on-site power mixers were kids like us who thought they were pretty grown up to be "in construction." The brick masons said it would build muscles and character. They sure were nice to help us grow up that way.

Mixing mortar was done in a flat wooden tub about 4'x8' and maybe 12" deep. The power mixer consisted of a shovel and a hoe with two holes in the blade. After shoveling a pile of sand into the tub, you mixed in the dry concrete from bags. When it was pretty evenly mixed, one of you hosed in water while the other mixed that heavy, slushy stuff together until you had MORTAR. That was hard, back-breaking work. The first batch was just work. The second, third, and fourth batches became torture. Fortunately, we were too numb to count after that.

The adults assured us the pain would go away. They said it was good for us to learn how to work together, help others, and see the results of our efforts. They may have been right. Our generation did learn how to work together, for the good of others, and an appreciation of the results of our efforts. We learned responsibility and respect.

I grew up still skinny, but with a lot of good memories. Like that hot summer day in 1935, mixing that heavy, thick mortar.

Someone came to the building site and told us they heard over the radio that Will Rogers and Wiley Post had crashed somewhere in Alaska!

To a boy of 11 who had as his heroes men like the Wright brothers, Charles Lindbergh, and Wiley Post, this was devastating. I had dreams of being like aviator Wiley Post, flying higher than the eagles, chasing the wind, soaring, and playing in the clouds. Now he had crashed way up in the wilds of Alaska. I remembered when Charles Lindbergh flew over the Atlantic Ocean. I remember hearing of the exploits of Wiley Post. Now he was gone! True, Will Rogers was gone, too. But my hero chased the clouds, just like I wanted to do.

Memories. Hard work. Dreaming. Fun and sadness. Role models. All part of growing up. Even though I became a military pilot in WWII, I still had flashbacks of one of the reasons I pursued and persisted in that goal. It was my memories of that hot summer day in 1935 when I heard of the fate of Will Rogers and Wiley Post.

Snow Camping

November 10, 2003

IN 1936, I JOINED the Boy Scouts of America. I was 12 years old, the required entry age back then. After a poor experience in one troop, I joined another. Troop 105, located at the Baptist Church on Main Street, Johnson City, New York, was sort of a rag-tag troop led by Scoutmaster Clifford Springer.

We all called him Cliff. Real disciplined type of group of boys, we were. Cliff was a bit overweight and full around the middle, balding, and easy-going. Wore glasses, didn't smoke, had no uniform at the time, but all the boys loved and followed Cliff. He was jolly, but meant what he said. He was fair and played no favorites.

As to uniforms, we boys wore uniforms made up of World War I surplus. At least those of us who could scrounge bits and parts from who knows where. But we all wore neckerchiefs alike. We were Troop 105 and proud of it.

Today, people would laugh at some of us with lace-up leggings, ammunition belts to carry flint and steel kits to build fires, first-aid items, scout knives, maybe a whistle for signaling, and other paraphernalia. Over the course of a few years, the effects of the depression were easing, and, with many of us boys able to get small part-time jobs (I delivered grocery store handbills for 50c per week), we managed to get a better-uniformed troop. Much of our equipment was still WWI vintage, and I even made my own sleeping bag, backpack, and pack frame.

The 1930s were years of learning to make do, make, or do without. But it made Troop 105 a great Troop. Cliff led us on to be among the toughest competitors at local camporees and jamborees. We learned how to camp out in the great out-of-doors.

Our sponsoring church owned a tract of land seven miles north of the village of Johnson City. It had a one-room cabin on the 14-acre tract, set well off the 2-lane road, nestled among farms and mostly covered by rolling woodlands. We were not restricted to just that property, because the farmers in the area knew the church and our troop would respect the environment.

For about three years, I hiked those seven miles to and from the camp almost every other weekend--- rain, sunshine, or snow. How I thank my parents for trusting me to have those experiences. Sometimes we stayed in the cabin if it was too wet and cold. We slept outdoors when the temperatures were right. Most of us did not have tents. Our meals were either cooked over a campfire or, on some occasions, inside. But the best times were camping in the snow.

SNOW? Why would I want to sleep out in the snow?! Let me explain.

The secret to living outdoors is to stay dry and as warm as possible. Snow is wet, but if you get wet, dry off. If you are cold, get to the best shelter possible. I grant you, sometimes these conditions are not correctable. But proper preparation and proper actions can make for a great experience.

Because we were in a wooded area, we had plenty of firewood. So we would build a nice fire outside the area where we had decided to make our lean-to. This helped keep us warm as we built our winter retreat. Also, in the woods, we would find that nature provides plenty of downed trees, big limbs, and, in that part of the country, pine boughs. When we arrived at camp, we would find a site where we would find a downed tree. It was easy enough to erect a lean-to between a couple of standing trees. If we wanted, we could lash the lean-to together. But sometimes we used our great "engineering" skills and made the frame to support itself. Then we would lace limbs over the framework so we could cover that with pine boughs. A roof like that would stand up under rain, wind, or snow. The pine boughs had to be layered so any moisture would travel down to the back of the lean-to and never run inside. That is, if you placed your lean-to in the right position so water would run around--not through-- where you plan to sleep and live.

A mattress is required wherever you plan to get a good night's sleep. After we got rid of as much snow as possible, we would pile a thick mat of fragrant pine needles inside the lean-to "floor" of our winter retreat. You now have a fine woodsman's mattress. (I can almost smell the pine needles now!)

Of course, we kept the fire fed. It being placed facing our lean-to opening, the heat provided all the warmth we needed. All through the night, whoever thought it was getting chilly simply reached over to the stack of firewood and kept the fire going. If rain or snow was falling, or expected, we would extend the roof out a bit when we did the building, and also built a covering for our fuel supply. Besides, the fire would be ready for use in the morning when we could cook eggs, bacon, toast, or even pancakes. After all, we didn't have far to go to get to our "refrigerator."

After a Hunter's stew supper, or whatever, we would crawl into our cozy home, remove our shoes and prop them up to dry overnight, shed whatever clothes you had nerve enough to shed, and head for bed. A sleeping bag, a full belly, and fire to keep you warm are but a memory now. But at the time, I found *Snow Camping* was the greatest challenge, the most fun, and the most rewarding camping of my boyhood years.

A Heel Of A Story

FEBRUARY 26, 2004

When I was at the ripe old age of seventeen, I decided to find a full-time job for the summer. We got out of school by the end of May and didn't start back until after Labor Day. That meant three months to start earning my way in this big old world.

My parents thought it was a good idea. I had finished my junior year of High School and would graduate the following January, at seventeen. It was 1940. Having gone through the Great Depression, our family was getting back to some normalcy financially, but it would be a help to earn some money of my own.

My Dad worked for the Endicott-Johnson Shoe Co. as a ladies' shoe designer and stylist. He had some connections with the people at the Vulcan Heel Co., located in Johnson City, NY, where we lived. So he suggested I try to get employment there. I put in an application, and I got the job!

Summertime set in about the first part of June, and by July, it got pretty warm. August was always hot. However, mornings were still quite cool until the sun came up to warm the factory where I worked. So, when I went to work each morning, it was very often cold. Especially under that big metal-roofed building. However, I was young, a big hunk of a 115-pound,

5'10, skinny kid. But hey, I was working a 40-hour-a-week job, which was pretty good for 1940.

And the pay was great!!! I made minimum wage of 35c per hour!!! Sure beat my previous job of delivering grocery store sales flyers at 50c per week. Even after they took out 1% Social Security, I took home $13.86. Yep! I was contributing 14c each week toward my old age retirement!!!

When I reported for work that first chilly morning at 6:45, I was told that because I liked to work with wood, I would work on the sanding belts to finish the wooden heels for ladies' shoes. (Don't try to say that last sentence too fast!!!) Sure enough, I was led to a bench that held a couple of motorized sanding belts, each belt a different width. My job was to take the pre-shaped wooden heels and give them a final sanding before they were sent to another department to be coated and receive rubber tips. After a brief demonstration by the man in charge, I was on my own. Wow!!! I was now a working man!!!

The thrill of learning and working blotted out the chill and the sawdust that was being generated as I sanded those wooden heels. I had a large bin of raw heels, but pretty soon I got the hang of how to smooth them down, and I sanded away, happy as a lark. It seemed like no time at all when the lunch whistle sounded.

Back then, there were no dining rooms, vending machines, or the types of trucks that bring sandwiches and such to work sites. If you wanted to eat, you brought your lunch from home in a metal lunch "pail." Your drink was in a thermos bottle inside the lid of the metal lunchbox. My mother fixed me a sandwich, sometimes adding an apple or a banana. My drink very often was lemonade (made at home), or homemade root or birch beer. No, it was not alcoholic. My mother and we three brothers made, from scratch, our own refreshing "soft drinks" because there were very few commercial types of cola. (The only one I remember was Coke, at 25c for six bottles. If you returned the glass bottles, you got 2c each.) I do not remember the formula of our drinks, or how they were mixed, but I fondly remember bottling and capping that homemade root beer and birch beer with my family.

After our brief lunch break, we went back to work. By then, the sun had heated the metal roof of the factory, which was rather low-built and windowless. There were a few strategically placed huge fans that tried to suck out some of the flying sawdust. Also, each sanding machine had a crude collection system that re-circulated rather than eliminated the sawdust. Other operations in the factory contributed to the amount of debris floating in the air. Chipping wood blocks into roughly shaped heels, and even the finishing products to coat the formed heels, floated everywhere.

Add to these conditions the noise of chippers, lathes, sanders, fans, and the total noise of people working as they moved materials and products.

Now add to this the heat. We did not perspire. We SWEAT !!! The further into the day we worked, the hotter it got under that metal roof. I remember the water fountain where we could get a drink. That is, if you could find time to take a break. As soon as my bin of heels was done, another full one appeared.

This sounds like a negative story. It is not. I went to work every morning, feeling like I was growing up. None of us complained about conditions. We had a job. We were earning our own way. We knew the value of each dollar we earned. We faced each day, as it was, not trying to make it something more. Good, honest, hard work.

I worked at the heel plant until the end of the summer, when school resumed after Labor Day. L-a-b-o-r D-a-y indeed.

These good memories make this into *A Heel Of A Story*.

Bridge, Anyone?

April 21, 2004

I met Caroline on August 26, 1944, had a long courtship, and then married her on October 8, 1944. Not long after that, I was shipped overseas during World War II. (In case you are a mathematician who insists on details, that was a courtship of six weeks. I fell in love when I met Caroline on a blind date and married her six weeks later.) I was 20 years old.

I went into the Army Air Corps shortly after I became 18 years old. I did not have a chance to go to college, where I am sure I would have learned those all-important social graces, such as playing bridge. Becoming a Second Lieutenant pilot polished off some of the rough edges, but that did not include dating girls, how to drink tea with your "pinky" in the air, or how to play bridge. (If we didn't already know about dating girls, we would never have been accepted as pilots!)

Bridge was not in the curriculum.

Just before being shipped out, Caroline suggested, if I got the opportunity, that I learn to play bridge, and she would go to the Officers Club to learn the game, too. Then we would have something to do when I got back. (That was not quite what I was thinking would be my first priority when I got back!!!) But I agreed. "Yes, Dear."

In India, we were assigned to four-man tents. We would daily check the flight schedules to see when we would fly from the Assam Valley in northeast India, over or around the Himalayan Mountains to various places in China. Once in a while, all four of us would be "at home" at the same time. It may be mid-day or mid-night, but every few days, we managed to be together. It takes four to have a table of bridge. Even if the table is a rickety reed square on bamboo legs.

Four guys from all walks of life sat around that table: A.B. (Red) Guthrie from Virginia, Dave Harris from Connecticut, Charles (Charlie) Hon from Tennessee, and myself from North Carolina. (Yes, I had grown up in New York state, but my wife and daughter lived in North Carolina. That was home for me.) Charlie was the only one who knew how to play BRIDGE!!!

Charlie was very patient with us. He taught us "real" bridge. During the learning period, we naturally had to discuss, rehash, and review our games. Over the months, we began to understand the finessing, cross-trumping, and the nuances of "psyching out" our opponents. We learned "real, he-man" bridge. Eventually, we got to where we did not sit and moan or groan over a goof or mistake. We went on to the next hand and learned from our mistakes. Time was important between missions, and we tried to make the most of it. We learned when to be aggressive and take our chances. It was great fun. I looked forward to sitting at a table with my bride and playing this game with her friends. But I was sure I could never learn well enough to keep up with those people who had been playing this game for years.

After my 72 ½ missions overseas, and I was back home with Caroline, I guarantee you that playing bridge was not on my list of first-things-first. Eventually, we thought it would be nice to invite friends over for a night of bridge. Yeah! Just what I was waiting for!!!

That evening came. We sat down for a great night of fast-moving, no-nonsense bridge with these friends. I was almost in a sweat. Could I keep up with this fine young couple that Caroline had known all her life, but I had just recently met? Maybe our little daughter would need my attention. (Some excuse.)

The cards were dealt. The bidding progressed. I have no idea now what was bid, but the hand was played. The first indication of what followed was, in between bids, there were comments about children, work problems, housing, etc. After the last card was played, I was waiting for the proper person to pull the cards together so we could get on with the next game. Instead, it was necessary for us to review each play, amid more conversation about current events and the cost of groceries.

Finally, we were dealt another hand. The same thing happened again. Here I was, expecting to be embarrassed about my inexperience and incompetence. Instead, I wondered why we were not playing bridge.

That was my indoctrination into what I had missed in my formative years of social grace training. But I learned fast. Bridge comes in many forms. I was not about to want to go back to India to play "real, he-man" bridge, so I learned how to be patient and play the social way. It really is fun this way, but it would be fun to once again have a game with Charlie, Red, and Dave. For old times' sake. Bridge, anyone?

Breaking Away

JUNE 7, 2002

No matter how much you love your parents or in-laws, there comes a time when you must declare your independence and assume the responsibilities of the family that you have established when you marry. And have children.

This is in no way a form of reflection on parents. Even if you stay in the same neighborhood with parents, at some point, it is necessary to have the privacy of your own "castle."

This is my opinion. Perhaps you are the exception. If so, great. Don't read any further.

The reason I express this opinion is to establish, for my own family, why they lived in the states of New York, North Carolina, Florida, South Carolina, and back into North Carolina. That is, until they married and, in turn, broke away.

After WWII was over, and I had returned to these wonderful United States of America, I naturally went to Wilmington, NC, where Caroline lived with her parents. While I was overseas, Caroline had our first child, Sharyn Elizabeth. However, having been born and raised in South Central New York State, my roots were there. Besides, I had another tie to that little village of Johnson City.

Having been employed by IBM in March of 1942, just after graduating from High School in January of that year, they paid me a week's wage every month that I was in service. I had enlisted in the Army Air Corps and was sworn in on December 4, 1942. Because of the generosity of IBM, I felt obligated to return to work with them. So Caroline, daughter Sharyn, and I lived in the state of NY for about a year and a half. Then we decided to move back to Wilmington, NC. Besides, Caroline was expecting our second child.

On November 15, 1947, our son Rick (RWT, Jr.) was born. He never really lived in NY, but at least he was conceived in that state.

During the twelve years of our family life in Wilmington, our son Rick was born. Then, eight years later, we were blessed to have our third child, Nancy. Our family was complete. But it was time for me to get out "on my own." There was great comfort to have Caroline's parents and relatives around us. But I felt I needed to "do my own thing," whatever that was. I turned down a flying career. After trying a couple of other ventures, such as my own photoengraving and art business, working in a toy store, etc. I decided to "break away" into a career that I loved. Our North Carolinian family was about to change allegiance to another state. I applied for full-time work with the Boy Scouts of America. Even at 35 years of age, I was accepted. At the training school for professional Scout Executives in Mendham, NJ, I was called "Dad."

Upon becoming a full-time Scouter, serving as a District Scout Executive, you agree to being moved from assignment to assignment roughly every three years, because there were only about 3500 of us to cover the USA and International posts. This meant the Turner household would do a lot of packing and repacking. Sharyn was 14, Rick almost 12, and Nancy was only 4 years old.

My first assignment was to the Blue Ridge Council, BSA, headquartered in Greenville, SC. My family would live in Anderson, SC, serving the surrounding areas. This meant our children became South Carolinians.

There are fond memories of Anderson: Nancy chasing our pet dog Susie in snow deeper than Susie was tall; Sharyn in that snow in a bathing suit, just like Caroline had done when she attended Louisburg College years earlier; Rick joining the Boy Scouts and being part of the annual camp-out in the city square, and getting flooded out by a tremendous overnight cloudburst.

So much for being SC citizens. Our next move was to the Sunshine State of Florida. My assignment was with the Gulf Ridge Council, BSA, headquartered in Tampa, FL. We lived in Lakeland, FL. Nancy started school. Caroline had the experience of watching Nancy "disappear into the mist" each morning, to be picked up by the school bus on the corner. (There were mornings when the mist, or light fog, almost shrouded the kids as they went to meet their bus.) Nancy learned that Christmas trees were not free.

In those years, Rick became an Eagle Scout, he learned to drive, probably noticed girls were different than boys, and when we moved to our next assignment, he stayed behind to finish his last six weeks of his sophomore year of high school. He stayed with the Dyches family next door. They had to be wonderful friends. (They still are.)

Sharyn had finished high school and started her college education at Florida State in Tallahassee. She had already found out that boys were different than girls in high school, and had her own car to take to college. (How those kids grew up!!!)

There are many other memories, but this narrative is to refresh the family about the geographical changes in our lives.

We spent five years in Lakeland, FL, longer than any other BSA scouter. When we left, Caroline and I were presented the keys to the City of Lakeland by the Mayor at a ceremony. I often wondered why they gave them to us as we LEFT. I never found out what those keys would open. But off we went, back to the state of South Carolina.

I served the Yamassee District, a part of the Georgia-Carolina Council, BSA. Augusta, GA, was the headquarters city, but we lived in Aiken, SC.

Again, I served that district longer than any other D.E. No city key was presented, but we accumulated great friends and memories.

Rick graduated from high school and went into the Air Force. Sharyn graduated from Florida State with a Master's degree and moved to Dallas, TX. Rick married and was assigned to Albuquerque, NM. Nancy learned there is a difference between girls and boys. She dated several, but must have really impressed one in particular. Read on.

Then came the day of returning to become North Carolinians again. By now, there were only three of us left to move. This time to the Mecklenburg County Council, BSA. We lived in the headquarters city of Charlotte, NC.

It was there that Nancy had every weekend visits from that boy that she knew in Aiken, SC. Jeff drove from Aiken to Charlotte every chance he got. Nancy had a most unusual wedding. When one of Jeff's sisters went to get the car for the newlyweds, she got hit. No injuries, but no car. Guess whose new car got "decorated" so the bride and groom could go on their honeymoon!!! Luckily, we had a second car. That was one way to "break away" from the family!

So, kids, now you know why you lived in so many states. It was so your parents could establish their own lives. In the process, we moved. I do not think it hurt any of you. In fact, I think it helped you, Sharyn, living in Plano, TX; you, Rick, living in Ft. Mill, SC; and you, Nancy, living in West Richland, WA. You may someday realize that you have done the same thing we did way back in 1959, and your kids may do the same as you when they feel the need, not to leave parents by getting away, but leaving by that urge for *Breaking Away*.

Art Development

May 23, 2002

When Caroline and I moved into our own home at 2217 Plaza Drive in Wilmington, NC, we began to settle down like we thought we should. Three children, a pet dog, one car, and a life ahead. Sound sort of dull? No way did we feel that way. It was what we wanted. We had our family, were regular, active members of our church, and had lots of wonderful friends.

To fill some of our evenings, after the kids had gone to bed, we sat in our living room and enjoyed developing and pursuing "the finer things in life." Namely, Caroline and our upright piano, and me sitting in front of a canvas that was on my homemade easel, painting, as she continued her musical entertainment.

When we moved into our home, we were given an old upright piano, one that had belonged to Caroline's aunt. It was old, but we had it tuned, and it was very nice to hear Caroline play it. She had taken lessons when she was a young girl, and could play lots of songs "by ear", meaning without music. However, she could read music and play from musical scores, too. There was just one slight complication. Caroline played everything in B flat. Anything other than B flat sort of had to include a lot of "correcting" as she played that piece. It took a little getting used to, but I loved my Caroline so much that she could have walked all over the keyboard and it would have been beautiful music to me.

Caroline played the piano on those wonderful evenings as I sat painting. The kids were in bed, and Susie, our pet dog, would lie on the sofa. She must have enjoyed the music as much as I did, only occasionally opening one eye or twitching an ear, as Caroline would search for the right notes. It was pure contentment.

As for my contribution to this part of our family life, I painted with oils on canvases. On my 27th birthday, 1951, my parents sent me a set of oils. The set consisted of sixteen tubes of different colors of oil paint, a palette knife, a small bottle of turpentine, and a small bottle of paint thinner. Also, there were a couple of brushes and a palette. The pamphlet inside the nice aluminum box that held all of these items led me to believe I could become a Goya, Titian, Toulouse-Lautrec, or Michelangelo! Sure!

All of my life, I have had a sort of artistic ability. I must have inherited this from my Dad, who was a designer of ladies' shoes. Through the years, I had worked with pastels, black and white drawings, carved objects from many different materials, and even did a couple of watercolors. But OILS! This would open a whole new world of expression for me.

Let me put all of this together for you: family, piano, oil painting, and quiet evenings.

Some evenings, I would get out my easel and the set of oils in that nice aluminum box. After setting up the easel, I placed either a new canvas or a painting that I had already started on it. Then I put my ashtray stand beside my favorite big easy chair, and settled in for a night of *Art Development*.

Caroline would finish her household chores, we would get the kids down, and then she would join me in the living room. How she loved to play that old upright. It seemed to be a form of relaxation for her. Mostly, she enjoyed playing hymns, and we would both try to sing along. Neither of us was opera material. Not even church choir material. But for each other on those evenings, we became STARS of musical melodies!!!

It wasn't until the 60s that the scientists and medical people connected smoking to the cause of cancer. When I graduated from high school, I started smoking a pipe. So we gave it no thought about the influence of tobacco smoke in our home. I smoked my pipe and sometimes Camel cigarettes. There were no filters on cigarettes back then, either. Mmm. Those Camel cigarettes were good smokin'. And a pipe full of Sr. Walter Raleigh sure provided an "air" of contentment. Now you know why I kept the ashtray stand beside my chair on those special evenings. (Incidentally, I quit smoking Nov. 15, 1969, 33 years ago, as of this writing.)

If the neighbors had any problems with all of this, they never told us.

There we were, Caroline playing the piano and Susie trying to get a nap. I would fill the air with the sweet aroma of good tobacco, attempting to create masterpieces from canvas and my set of oils. We sometimes sang off-key, and Caroline occasionally hit a few notes that made Susie shift position or go to another room. Either the kids slept through all of this, or they buried their heads in the pillows. Odd how they have never mentioned any of this to us through the years. Maybe they just laughed themselves to sleep!

The Turner household was anything but dull. Painting a picture on canvas to the accompaniment of a piano that sometimes needed prodding to get to the right notes — or even whole bars — filled many an evening with togetherness, laughter, love, and the fun of ART DEVELOPMENT.

Experiencing a Hurricane

FEBRUARY 20, 2004

THERE ARE MANY STORIES about the experiences of people who have lived through a hurricane. This story is about the Turner family and Hurricane Hazel that hit Wilmington, NC, on October 15, 1954.

Hurricanes came ashore all up and down the East Coast of the United States throughout history. But seldom did they strike Wilmington, NC, and the beautiful beaches that are located south of the Outer Banks. Wilmington, located up the Cape Fear River, seemed fairly protected over the years. But Hurricane Hazel caught many by surprise. It not only hit up and down the coast; it came ashore with a pent-up fury, right into Wilmington.

At the time, it was apparent the eye of the storm was going to hit around Wilmington, and I was on the third floor of the Atlantic Coast Line Office Building on Front Street, downtown. I was employed in the Timekeeping Department of the ACL Railroad, where the payrolls were handled. I remember looking out the windows and seeing the roofs on the riverfront warehouse buildings suddenly being lifted into the air and disintegrating mid-air. The storm had not yet arrived, but the outer bands of clouds and air currents had. It was about quitting time, so people decided to go home a little early. Besides, those large windows of our building seemed to vibrate.

As I left the building, it shocked me to see one of the "No Parking" signs out front being whipped around like a whip. The winds were really picking up. Thankfully, our carpool all got home safely.

When I arrived home, Caroline, about three months pregnant with our third child (back then we did not have the ability, nor would we want, to determine that the baby would be a Nancy), waited with Sharyn and Rick, ages 10 and 7 respectively. The winds were roaring, but the eye of the hurricane was still down the coast and unpredictable. We felt fairly safe.

Having been a Boy Scout as a boy, and an Eagle, I had been a volunteer adult leader with the local District and Council for the past few years. Knowing there was time before any disaster, if any, would arrive, I contacted the local BSA officials and volunteered to go downtown to the shelter that would be set up for any storm victims. When I arrived, I found the National Guard had already delivered piles of army cots and bedding. But no one had set up these supplies. A couple of other adult scouters and I got the cots set up and sort of organized. Eventually, the Red Cross people arrived, and we left.

Back home and in many places in the city, there was a loss of electricity. It was our good fortune to have a gas range, so we knew Caroline could at least cook, have hot water, and heat the house—providing the gas lines held. (If they ruptured, maybe we wouldn't need food, water, and heat!)

But many others in the neighborhood were not as fortunate. Our next-door neighbor had an all-electric house, but no power. However, Dob, the nickname for the man next door, was a ham radio operator with a huge gasoline generator in his garage. It was fine as an emergency backup for his powerful radio set-up, but he could not heat, cook, etc., because he did not want to run out of fuel for emergencies.

So Caroline did the cooking while Dob became the only contact with the outside world. By sharing food supplies and coffee, our two homes became Central Headquarters during Hurricane Hazel!!!

That first night was the time they expected the eye to maybe come near Wilmington. Caroline had an aunt and uncle who lived on Harbor Island on the Inland Waterway. Some phone lines were still up, so Caroline confirmed through relatives in town that her aunt and uncle were still on the island. She wondered if it would be possible to get to them and "rescue" these elderly, long-time residents who may or may not know the danger that was approaching them. Guess who volunteered to go to the island to check on them?

I cannot remember who, but another adult agreed to go with me. In my car, we headed into the eye of the hurricane. (Doesn't that sound heroic?!!!) It was not, because we still were not sure if the eye would come ashore there, or when. Anyhow, we drove toward the island. In order to get to the island, it would be necessary to cross a bridge, of course.

As we approached the bridge, we saw flashing red lights. We stopped. The Highway Patrolman stepped over to our car and said we could go no farther. Why were we out in this weather, anyway? I explained our mission. He was very sympathetic. But told us we would have to turn around and go home. No one would be able to go over the bridge. It was unsafe, and anyone on the island would have to ride out the storm. Everyone had been warned, and some had refused to leave. Caroline's aunt and uncle were two of several who would not leave. Not wanting to get any wetter with my window down, and the patrolman seeming to be a nice guy, I decided to go back home instead of to a jail cell. Home we went, through some of the hardest rainfall I had seen since flying the monsoons over the Himalayan Mountains in WWII.

It turned out that the aunt and uncle had water in their house up to the keyboard of their piano. But they survived. The next time a hurricane came through, they were some of the first to evacuate!

Back home, we all gathered on the back porch of Dob's house, where his radio equipment was housed. By now, there had gathered more "Ham" radio operators who wanted to relieve Dob, because now the full force of the storm was about to hit Wilmington, NC. And hit, it did.

All communication to the outside world was cut off to and from Wilmington, except through the radio setup on the back porch of our next-door neighbor. He and other operators worked for a couple of days around the clock, dispatching trains from Rocky Mount and other cities, making requests for needed supplies, and sending messages to relatives through other radio "hams." Reports to news media went through this station.

Naturally, our children remember some of this, and they tell me about their impressions the morning after the storm blew over and away. Our only damage was the loss of a few shingles and a portion of the picket fence around our back yard. But one house down the street had a big pine tree completely split the roof in half, leaving the trunk suspended across the walls. All sorts of debris and damage were evident in our neighborhood. I will not attempt to give a report on the devastation from Hurricane Hazel. That can be found in the library.

This was the first natural disaster experience we had as a family. We went through four other hurricanes as a family in North and South Carolina, and Florida. I saw my first real tornado in New Mexico. Caroline and I went through one tornado together in an automobile. Hurricane Hugo really clobbered us in NC. We served as employees of the Red Cross when that hit. 12 days without power were quite an experience. As a teenager, I experienced the effects of the flooding after a cloudburst. The results of an ice jam that broke in the river where we lived showed the awesome power of flooding waters a couple of years later.

So I count my blessings and trust my Lord to protect my loved ones and me. But this is my story of living through a real-life hurricane, named Hazel.

VW "BUG" vs CADILLAC

Februrary 9, 2004

One summer, Caroline, my wife, and Nancy, our youngest child, decided to take a vacation trip. We would travel by automobile. Namely, a Volkswagen sedan affectionately referred to as a "Bug."

A Volkswagen sedan is a four-passenger, rear-engine, four-cylinder-powered German-built automobile. Those of us who owned one considered it the finest car on the road. Well, one of the finest. At least some of us did. It was very fuel-efficient, maneuverable, rugged, and quite comfortable. The only drawback was that it was not the largest car on the road. In size, that is. I guess it all depends on the size of the people, but we have traveled with six people. But not more than a one-day trip.

It was amazing how much could be packed in one of these little automobiles. Because the engine was in the rear, the only thing under the bonnet, or hood, was the ten-gallon gas tank. The rest of the space was the trunk. (Why not? The elephant has its trunk up front!!! I'm not sure about its engine.)

Our route would include a stop in Columbus, Ohio, to see my brother Hank and his wife and family. From there, we would go down to Louisville, Kentucky, to visit our long-time friends, Bo and Lib Dyches. Then we would find our way back home to Aiken, South Carolina.

We toured along the highways in our little ole VW, big as anyone else on the road. Just the three of us, enjoying the scenery and good weather. We thoroughly felt at ease and relaxed as we headed for Ohio. At times, other vehicles would pass us. And at other times, we would pass other vehicles. We respected them, and they respected us. That is, until we approached a ramp where a road intersected the main highway on which we were traveling.

We had traffic all around us, front and back, and beside us. Approaching the ramp was a great big white Cadillac. The driver entered the ramp and didn't seem to want to slow down!

It became evident that Mr. Cadillac thought he was bigger than the little blue VW, and he was going to cut us off. Well, I did not have too much choice. I could slow down and create a traffic problem behind us. Or I could keep my speed and hope the "farmer jerk---that is a family joke that goes way back to my Dad---would decrease his speed.

Imagine our little VW going along in the traffic, minding our own business, suddenly being attacked by a big ole white Cadillac that was trying to cut us off.

Maybe my ugly horns popped out, but I was determined not to let that happen. I did not want to endanger my family, but neither did I want to cause a pile-up behind us. So I kept my little VW going straight ahead, letting that big Caddy know I was as big as he was and he could not invade my space. I glanced over and realized the driver was a bit disturbed that I would not yield to him.

Suddenly, the Caddy driver realized he was running out of ramp. So he finally had to bring the contest to a screeching halt. He overran the end of the ramp a bit, but it served him right.

I halfway expected the surrounding traffic to break out in horn-honking applause, but it didn't happen. That was ok. We taught that big ole white Cadillac not to mess around with our neat little ole light blue VW.

Over The Fence

May 15, 2004

WHAT ARE FRIENDS FOR if they cannot help each other in times of need? This is a story about next-door neighbors who carried this old axiom to the limit. After you read this, you will understand how deep friendship can be, or burst out laughing about how foolish some people can be in the name of good Samaritanship. (That is a new word I just invented!!!)

In early 1961, my family and I moved to Lakeland, Florida. There, I became the District Executive for the Boy Scouts of America, with Council headquarters in Tampa. We lived in Lakeland and served the Lakeland-Plant City District. Later, it became necessary to split the service area because of our large growth. We re-named ourselves the Great Thunderbird District, serving Lakeland.

Sometime in 1962 or 1963, a new family moved next door to us. We became instant best friends, and still are to this day. Their names were Bo and Lib Dyches. The first morning they were in their new home, my wife Caroline put on a fresh pot of coffee and prepared eggs, bacon, etc. for breakfast. She had the kitchen window open wide, and the odors wafted out of the window in the direction of our new neighbors. (If you knew Bo, you would realize he could smell good food cooking within several blocks.) As I recall, we carried the food next door. We did not have far to go because Bo was seen standing out front with his nose testing the odors that drifted toward his house. Needless to say, we all became very close friends, children, and all.

Our children were a little older than the Dyches children, but not by much. In fact, our Nancy and their Beth were about the same age. They played together and went to school together. They had the same love of music and sang together. They bonded well.

In 1963, I built a playhouse for Nancy. It was made of scrap pieces of 2x4s, pieces of Masonite scrounged from the construction of the new homes in our new development, and rusty nails. It had a main room with surround windows (meaning no sills or windows) and a front porch consisting of a couple of 2x4 pillars and a railing. Overall, it must have measured about four by eight feet. It stood maybe six feet high- in places. The floor was real, natural sand. There was no need for a door because we had no hinges. Besides, we had nothing to make into a door.

Crude as it was, it was a playhouse, and the neighborhood kids had lots of fun in, out, and around Nancy's "home away from home." In fact, it was the envy of the kids in the area. (That is one way to keep track of your kids!!!)

In 1964, I received an opportunity to gain new experiences in my career when I was offered a new position with the BSA in Aiken, SC. This meant packing up our household and moving. But in no way could we take Nancy's playhouse with us. What should we do with it?

Bo Dyches was a representative of Chevron Oil Co. and had many contacts with a great variety of people. One such person was a retired Methodist missionary who had served in Cuba. Somehow it came about that Bo was given a deed from the missionary friend to some acreage on the Isle of Pines south of Cuba. It had been a Methodist Youth Camp, was covered with stands of pine trees, and had quarries of marble. A total of 80 acres was given to Bo. (I never asked him why. Sometimes it is wise not to ask too many questions — for the sake of friendship, or personal and family safety.) Bo seemed completely satisfied that the gift was legitimate, so I believed him. (What are friends for?!!!)

Bo said he would like to trade the playhouse for 10% of his holdings on the Isle of Pines in Cuba. Fidel Castro had taken over the Island and converted it into a military training camp, so the deed was and would be rather worthless. But now you begin to see how deep our friendship was. He wanted that playhouse for his daughter, and I had always wanted to own an island. The deed was worthless, but so was that scrap material run-down shack of a playhouse. Neither of us ever looked back on these arrangements with each other, but again, this was and still is a very deep friendship. We agreed to the deal.

However, being such close friends, it was decided to draw up a legal document of transfer of the two properties and real estate. Somewhere there exists such a legal document, notarized and witnessed. I got my island property, and Bo got the playhouse. If I ever find a copy, I will share it with you. It is hilarious. The party of the first part---etc!!! There were just a few minor details still to be worked out.

Each of the homes on Park Drive in Lakeland, Florida, had a chain-link fence dividing all of the properties. The fences were about 4 ½ to 5 feet high. The playhouse would have to be moved next door into the backyard of the Dyches' property. It would be costly to cut into the fence and then repair it. That meant OVER THE FENCE. Wow!

Thanks to Bo's son, Paul, our son Rick, a few neighbors with strong backs, and, of course, my supervision, the playhouse was lifted, moved over the fence, and put in place in the backyard of the Dyches family. It is a miracle that it held together, but apparently, my great skill as a playhouse builder survived the test.

We moved to SC, and soon after, the Dyches moved to Kansas City. After many years and moves on the part of both families, we have both ended up in South Carolina. They, in Aiken, and I in Ft. Mill--- Caroline having made the greatest move of all when she went to be with her Sweet Jesus in 2000. But of all the moves we have made, the one that gave us great love and laughter was when we moved the playhouse from our backyard to theirs---*Over The Fence*.

BURNING STICK COFFEE

DECEMBER 5, 2003

THERE COMES A TIME in many people's lives when a steaming cup of coffee seems to be all that is necessary to get from one moment to the next.

Add to that cold weather, a campfire, and a group of men around that campfire, good conversation, and every breath making these men look like steam engines. Most of them have finished a meal prepared over an open fire, just about like the one that is about to give these men some famous *Burning Stick Coffee.*

I did not originate this type of coffee preparation, but I do take credit for having introduced it to hundreds of adult Boy Scouts of America leaders in Florida, Georgia, and North and South Carolina. I was a professionally trained District Scout Executive serving in the Blue Ridge, Gulf Ridge, Georgia-Carolina, and Mecklenburg Councils of the BSA. In this capacity, I, with volunteer adult leaders, developed myriad outdoor programs for the boys and their leaders, many of which were held out-of-doors.

Usually, in the spring and fall, we held what was called a Camporee. These competitive, instructional, and fun-filled events lasted three days and two nights. After the men got the boys settled down and the camp was fairly quiet, the men would congregate around my headquarters area for talk, good-natured fun, and of course, a cup or mug of coffee. It was a time of great fellowship.

Sometimes, we developed training courses for the adults that may last for a whole weekend. Here again, in the evening, there would be a gathering around the headquarters campfire for more fellowship and comparing of experiences. And some of the greatest storytelling you have ever heard. Of course, there was the need for that pot of coffee.

Whenever I was transferred to a new assignment, I could hardly wait to introduce my method of preparing the coffee at the nightly campfire. I had learned it at the school for training we full-time Scouters, in Mendham, NJ, back in 1959, at the Schiff Scout Training Reservation.

In Lakeland, Florida, I found just the right coffee pot. It was an old-time conical-shaped, blue-speckled, wire and wood-handled pot with the snout on the side. It must have held at least two to three gallons. (I never did know exactly, because part of making this coffee is in scientifically measuring the approximate amounts.)

At the first outdoor event in my assignment in Lakeland, I set up my campsite, went about doing what I needed to do, and as night approached, I made sure there was a nice fire burning, with plenty of extra firewood for the evening. Sure enough, as the camp quieted down for the night, the adults drifted over for some fellowship. I had prepared my coffee pot by pouring in the exact approximate amount of water, sort of up to the bottom of the spout. I had very carefully added an exact, scientific, carefully measured approximate amount of ground coffee. (From a three-pound tin, you pour out the coffee down to somewhere near one of the rings of the can.) I was now ready to prepare coffee for this group of expectant men. That is, for coffee, naturally!

The fire was burning well, so I put the pot right in the middle of the fire. This got some attention. But it was when the lid of the pot started to pop up and down that I took the pot off the fire and let the brew settle. The men got curious when I put the pot back on the fire, and when the lid started to jump up and down quite steadily, they looked a little concerned. So I took the pot off the fire again and put it beside the fire to settle.

By now, the men thought it was time to serve that coffee. When I put the pot back on the fire the third time, some thought I had camp fever, or something. They had not seen anything yet!!!

Shortly, the lid of the pot was really jumping and was about to pop right off the pot into the fire. That is when I knew it was time to teach these men about BURNING STICK COFFEE. I took the pot off the fire, removed the lid, reached into the fire, and got a stick with lots of fire. I took that burning stick and put it into the pot of coffee and stirred it real good. Then I put the stick back in the fire, the lid on the pot, and said, "Gentlemen, your coffee is ready."

Well, their eyes popped like the pot lid popped. They looked at each other, made several comments, which I will not repeat, and wondered if I was trying to fool them. So, I got my cup, and after a few minutes had passed to be sure I had their attention, I poured me a cup of coffee and drank it, to prove it was drinkable. Slowly, these guys decided to try the burning stick brew. Then the chatter really got underway. They even made comments about how "bad" the coffee was. It must have been real "bad" because I had to make another pot of the stuff.

There were comments about having to strain the coffee between their teeth to keep from drinking the ashes. They wondered if it took special kinds of wood. How much water and coffee did I use? Sure was odd how they hated that coffee, gallon after gallon. Of course, the colder the weather, the more they would drink anything that was hot.

It was fun teaching men over those years, in many an evening around an open campfire. But it was a learning experience that most will never forget, as they recalled their first exposure to my *Burning Stick Coffee*.

A Trip To Philmont

PHILMONT SCOUT RESERVATION IS located in New Mexico, west of Springer, beneath the Tooth of Time Mountain in the Rocky Mountains, near Cimarron. Part of the Santa Fe Trail can still be seen on one of the many trails that make up this real wilderness experience for Boy Scouts who are able to take part.

Each expedition usually has 3 or 4 adult Scouters accompanying a group of anywhere from 10 to 20 boys. The boys are to be 14 years old or up to 18. They should have some outdoor camping and hiking experience. They will spend 12 days on the trail. Our total time for the travel and trail time will be 24 days.

Boy Scouts from all over the USA and some foreign countries come for the challenge of Philmont, a part of the Boy Scouts of America.

It was my opportunity to be part of the leadership of an expedition in 1968. I worked for the BSA as a District Executive in the Georgia Carolina Council headquartered in Augusta, GA. I served the Yamassee District and lived in Aiken, SC. My District was one of several served by the Council. The Council had hired a bus and driver to carry us on our trip. There were two volunteer adult Scouters, 18 boys, the driver, and myself. The driver, Bill, would not go on the trails.

The boys raised their money, got their equipment, and psyched themselves up for this once-in-a-lifetime experience. The men were all ready for the adventures ahead. It was time to get everyone together for a shake-down equipment and orientation meeting. We had to be sure each one had the required boots, clothing, tents, backpacks, canteens, etc. Also, we had to be sure they did not take excess items that would not be needed.

A most important reason to have this meeting, with parents required attendance, was to get to know each other before we ever got on the bus. Many of the boys knew each other, and some of the adults. But it was necessary for all of us to know what to expect when we got on the bus and then out on the trails. We emphasized the Boy Scout oath and laws. We also emphasized the patrol method of boy leadership, but the reasons why adults were there was to teach them respect for the out-of-doors, the fun and freedom of living with nature. We got off to a great start.

The day of departure arrived. The bus and Bill, the driver, arrived. Then the boys and parents arrived. I arrived. Where were the other two adults?!!!

We were informed that one man came down with some pains in his stomach. The other man broke his shoulder. As for me, I felt my heart drop to the bottom of my stomach!!! 18 boys stood there, dressed in Boy Scout uniforms with all their packs and gear; 36 eyes were trained on me with questions and concern. All those parents had sacrificed so much to give their sons this experience. There was my boss, other members of the Council staff, and my wife Caroline, all wondering what I would do.

Naturally, we would go to Philmont! But with only Bill the driver, and this 42-year-old little Boy Scout to lead them and be responsible for feeding, guiding, and tucking them in bed each night. We would sleep on gymnasium floors some nights, at naval air stations at least two nights, eat at fast food places, and take in tourist sites if possible. I would handle all the money, mediate any squabbles if they occurred, take care of homesickness if necessary, and be momma and papa for at least two weeks. With all of that fun in store, I decided to take this gang to Philmont. In retrospect, I think I was a little bit insane.

Before we boarded the bus, I made an announcement to all of the assembled boys, parents, and any other interested persons in attendance to the effect that " from the time we board this bus, you will have me as your father until we return. If you cannot respect this condition, do not board the bus. You will be my sons to discipline or praise, and I will try to be fair and respect you in return." We all boarded the bus. I guess I had suddenly adopted 18 sons!!!

Our first night out, we stayed at the Naval Air Station at Meridian, Miss. The Navy was great as a host. Some of the boys got to "fly" a jet simulator. Of course, knowing I had been a WWII pilot, they insisted I try to fly the simulator. After I crashed a couple of times, it was decided that it was well that the war was over!!! The next morning, we had breakfast at the base cafeteria. It cost us 10 cents each for all we could eat. (Ask me how many eggs, sausage, bacon, toast, pancakes, coffee, juice, grits, fruit, etc., yours truly ate. I am ashamed to put this in print!)

Our trip included a tour of Vicksburg. We saw the newly discovered ironclad "Cairo" that was raised in the Yazoo River. Crossed the great Mississippi River and spent the night at England Air Force Base in Alexandria, LA.

We toured the Alamo in San Antonio, TX, the next day before arriving at Randolph Air Force Base. Col. Davis and Captains Hollowell and Bierberstien demonstrated jet aircraft and night landings.

On June 15th, we entered Mexico at Del Rio, crossing the Rio Grande River Bridge. The boys enjoyed "talking down" the prices on souvenirs. That is where they purchased the Mexican motif set of bookends they presented to me at the end of the expedition. They were and still are a wonderful and cherished surprise. It was on our way to Pecos, TX, that we saw a tornado in the distance. It really kicked up the debris, and we were glad it was in the far distance. The sand storm was an experience, too. That night, we slept on a school gymnasium floor.

The next morning, we toured the Pecos Museum for a peek into Wild West history. On to Carlsbad Caverns for a 3 and ½ hour tour. We ate lunch 750 ft. below ground. Real impressive. At Walker Air Force Base, M/Sgt. Zuber gave the boys "Pecos Diamonds." Then to sleep.

Proceeding to Sandia Base, Albuquerque, NM, on June 17th, CWO Dustin almost followed suit and adopted 18 boys, as well. He gave them base privileges, including a swimming pool, TV, billiards, shuffleboard, softball, and free snacks.

On June 18th, we left Sandia Base and headed for our destination---Philmont!!! Great anticipation filled the air of our bus as we approached the small town of Springer, NM. As we crossed the river on the outskirts of this small town, we saw that the water was lapping at the girders of the bridge that we must cross. The town of Springer was flooded.

We passed through Springer and proceeded to French Corner, where we were to take the road east to the Reservation. In the distance, we could see the Tooth of Time, the landmark familiar to all who have been to Philmont. But during the night, there had been a big flash flood on the Cimarron River.

Then is when we heard we could not get to Philmont. The Reservation could not be reached from any direction because all of the bridges had been washed out. Radio communication via local police reported Philmont was closed to all expeditions until June 25th, and all those en route should return home. I got confirmation of this through the Sheriff Department and the State Highway Patrol. There was damage in the camps, and the water supply was contaminated.

Springer was a very small town, and a lot of people seemed to be stranded there. Most of them appeared to be transient migrant workers. Our big modern bus full of young boys with a lot of equipment may have been attractive to some of those people. The mayor of Springer asked me to have our group spend a couple of nights there and see if Philmont might open soon. It did not seem to be too safe, so I told him we were going back to Amarillo, Texas. We had the police contact Philmont to apprise them of our decision and destination. So off we went from that extremely hot, flooded town and headed east.

We had been on the road about an hour when a State Patrolman flagged us down, with a message from the Central Military Command, directing us to re-route ourselves to Amarillo Air Base for one night, and then to proceed to Dallas Naval Air Station, where they were expecting us to stay for a couple of nights. This was fine with me because we had already made some preliminary plans. Our home Council had been notified of our whereabouts and our immediate plans, so the parents could be reassured.

The boys were made aware of the situation at every step. Because I had had a crash graduate course in boy psychology in Springer, New Mexico, just an hour or so ago, I got the boys enthused in a full day at Six Flags Over Texas Theme Park. They helped plan who would make up three teams that would be on their own, using the Scout Patrol method. They elected leaders and when we would rendezvous at what times, so we wouldn't lose anyone. Having been to the Park a few years back with my wife, Caroline, and two of our children, I had enough knowledge to build enthusiasm for the fun these boys could expect.

The trip to the Park, the cordial welcome from Cdr. Brown and his aide in completing our return itinerary, and the wonderful meals made this part of our trip a great success.

The next day, we traveled to Barksdale Air Force Base, where Col. Mason greeted us. It so happened that our expedition leader (that's me) was stationed at this base 21 years prior, having been assigned as a pilot of B-26 medium bombers. A sort of homecoming.

Our final night of the trip was spent at Meridian Naval Air Station, Meridian, Miss. Chief Don Bundy let some of the boys "fly" the jet Link trainer again. Of course, there were a lot of crashes, but a lot of laughs, too. You might say it was a crashing finale to a great and most successful tour.

When we arrived back in Augusta, GA, the next day, June 23rd, the boys grinned, and some were embarrassed at being hugged and kissed by their mothers. But they were glad to be back home. Expressions like "remember when we---", " You should have seen---", and "It was awesome when---" were heard as the boys and their parents drove away.

A final note: On June 12th, 1965, you, the members of Expedition 618-B, left on a trip that could have been a precarious, disheartening experience. Bill, the bus driver, and I saw inches of growth in each of you as we all went forward in a true spirit of Scouting. I know you were disappointed, but it is to your credit that it did not show, and you accepted what had to be. You looked ahead to what the next day would hold forth, with a healthy anticipation.

All through the 12 days I spent with you, a group whom I never knew before, it was a pleasure to be a part of your experiences. In appreciation for your cooperation and excellent conduct, I can only say thank you for letting me watch each of you take a step toward becoming a man full-grown.

Shipwrecked

September 14, 2003

It was a beautiful summer day, back in the 1980s. Caroline and I were visiting her family in Wilmington, NC, where we had met, married, and had our three children. We had lived there for many years before I went to work for the Boy Scouts of America. It was "our hometown." Many of her family still lived there.

Caroline's cousin had a nice seaworthy fishing boat. He lived on Harbor Island, across the Inland Waterway from Wrightsville Beach. Being a close-knit family, this cousin invited his brother, Caroline's brother, and myself to go "outside" to do some fishing.

I have never been much of a fisherman, but had done some surf and pier fishing through the years with these men. So it was agreed we would go out and load the boat with a catch of some good blue fish and whatever else got in the way of our hooks and lines.

We four got aboard the boat and made our way into the waterway that led to Masonboro Inlet, south of Wrightsville Beach. If we could get through the currents of the inlet, we would then have fairly smooth passage to the fishing grounds of that part of the Atlantic Ocean. The waters there are warmed by the Gulf Stream and provide great fishing.

It was a bit rough as we plowed through the rough currents that flow into the coastal waterways along the eastern coast. But the two cousins were pretty good sailors, and we bounced through, hanging on for dear life. But once through, it was great. Except for a slight problem. The inboard engine started to cough and spit, and dark smoke started to billow out of the covering! Then some flames indicated we had a problem!

We were in the Atlantic Ocean, surrounded by all of that water, and we were on fire!

Our options seemed rather limited:

Jump overboard and swim what looked like half the distance of the Atlantic Ocean to dry land. (Who wants to abandon a nice boat like that---even if the engine was burning!)

Stay there and hope to splash enough water on that engine to put out the fire.

Yell loud and hope someone could hear and come rescue us. (There was not another boat within sight!)

Turn around and see who could win the race to shallow water--- the nerves of four guys in a burning boat or the burning boat.

We turned around. When we got close enough to shore to have to have swum, if necessary, to safety, the brothers were finally able to get the flames out, and most of the smoke was dying away. We must have looked like an old-time steamboat chugging across the waves to the people who had gathered on each side of the inlet.

Some people called out to us that they had alerted the Coast Guard Station when they saw the smoke way out there in the great Atlantic Ocean. The Coast Guard had a small cutter stationed just inside the inlet.

We got to the mouth of the inlet, and it was decided to beach, or run aground, the boat inside, rather than outside the inlet, because it was much easier to let the currents propel the boat to the safer, smoother waters. It was just inside the pushing, not so rough waves and currents, that our fishing trip ended as the cousins ran the boat up onto the sand. By now, all flames and smoke were gone, and we were safely on dry ground. Our fishing trip was sort of "dampened," but at least we were not still swimming around in the Gulf Stream.

It was as we stood around with a small gathering crowd of onlookers, that we looked out to the approaches of Masonboro Inlet and watched the Coast Guard boat on its way to save we poor fishermen who had been shipwrecked. Luckily, they saw our poor beached boat and did not have to go looking for us. But we wondered what took them so long!

Wouldn't it have made a great story if they had not seen us, went through the inlet, and searched and searched the big Atlantic for a burning fishing boat with four guys aboard? It would have made this shipwreck story rather insignificant in comparison.

Nudes vs Butterflys

April 28, 2004

It was a pleasure and blessing that Caroline, my wife and sweetheart, and I were able to travel to many places before she went on her final trip to be with her Sweet Jesus December, 7th 2000.

Our last cruise was a return to some of the islands in the Eastern Caribbean, and some that we had not visited before. Our cruise continued to South America and on through the Panama Canal. One stop was on the island of Martinique, a French Island.

We had heard there was a large butterfly farm inland on the island. Caroline loved butterflies and almost always wore a butterfly pin on the shoulder of her garments. (Except her nightgowns, of course. She was a very modest person.) Naturally, we would go to the butterfly farm.

Because Martinique is French, the beaches conform to the European code of beachwear: less is best. It was quite warm in that part of the world, so I felt it was important that we take a refreshing dip in the Atlantic Ocean. But there was a conflict of scheduling the swim at the same time as the trip to the butterfly farm. Caroline expressed her regrets about the conflict, but felt it would be more interesting to go into the hot jungle area to see butterflies than to go to the beach to see — swimmers and ocean waves.

Being a gentleman, and deeply in love with my own "butterfly" for over 55 years, I acquiesced to her wishes. (Either that or I could swim back to the

States.) I never could understand why she did not want to go swimming, but then, I may have had my own agenda!!! We signed up for the inland trip.

It was hot. But it was also very enlightening to ride past banana trees wrapped in their blue plastic covers, see the native way of living, hear about how the natives lived, see the natives at work (fully clothed), and finally get to the butterfly farm.

What a disappointment!!! The farm was quite large, as butterfly farms are concerned, but it was very crude. The enclosures were screen-wire ramshackle affairs. The place was muddy in places and altogether quite dirty. The displays were nowhere near what we expected, and the guide was not too well informed. Most of the display cases were not clean, and we saw a lot of dead butterflies!

We had been to similar live displays at Calloway Gardens in Georgia, Winter Haven, Florida, at the zoos in Alabama and North Carolina, and a couple of other places. These were truly beautiful displays of our winged friends. We were not impressed. But at least we had seen the Martinique version of a butterfly farm.

I often wondered if Caroline secretly wished she had gone for a swim or just smiled when I wasn't looking. The way I rationalized, after all, was why go looking for calico when you have silk at home. There are lots of butterflies, too, but only one Caroline.

Turner Tuna Recipe

January 30, 2004

Early in 2004, my daughter Sharyn asked if I had any favorite recipes to share in a project she had started. Or any favorite recipes that my sweet wife had prepared while she was still alive.

The second part of the request was easy. All of Caroline's recipes were super delicious, scrumptious, and good. Sharyn already had her mother's Red Velvet Cake recipe and a few others. Caroline was able to take any leftover food and make a great meal. So I could not help there.

As to the second part, she must have been having a nightmare. Or on the verge of one. Or would have if she tried to eat what I cook. (That word is misleading!) Since I lost Caroline, I depend on single-serve frozen foods, cereals, eggs, soups, etc. I am not an adventurous cook. I have a microwave oven, toaster oven, toaster, coffeemaker, and a George Foreman grill. I use my range for pizza, breakfast meals, and my SECRET FUDGE. The secret ingredient in my fudge recipe will be learned when they read my will. Unless I give it to my grandchildren before.

I am not a cook. But I do have one recipe that I will share with Sharyn: Tuna fish salad. The following is my recipe:

The quantities following must vary with the number of cans of tuna used. Try this first:

Two 6-ounce cans of light chunk tuna (use the tuna, not the cans) packed in spring water. You can use summer, fall, or winter, I guess. Squeeze out the water and remove from the cans. Put tuna in a mixing bowl. It is easier to mix if you use a bowl.

One hard-boiled aig, peeled. Chop the aig in small pieces, including the yaller part.

About a small handful (either hand) of chopped up sliced dill piggles.

One good handful (either hand) of chopped up white or yaller onyon.

Another handful (either hand) of chopped serry. About one stawk.

Mix all the stuff together in that bowl. Then add about 2 tablespoons of miyonase. Mix.

Add more too or less as you like it.

Six cans of tuna (not the cans) will require about 3 aigs, lots more piggles, onyon, serry, and miyonase.

Don't chop the stuff too fine. It is better crunchy.

Be sure to use a sharp knife, but don't cut your fingers. And don't leave any fingernails in the mix. If any is left over, be sure to put it in the icebox. Or refrigerator, if you have one.

This tuna salad makes a great samich. Or a tuna melt using Swiss cheese.

When you get enough nerve, try this recipe using a can of pink salmon. (Out of the can, of course.) Get wild and mix the tuna and the salmon. Catfish, shark, and crappie are not very good substitutes.

This recipe is submitted to my daughter for her project. It is in memory of my Caroline, who taught me everything I know. About making tuna fish salad, that is.

VERSE

A Pain In The Back

January, 1972

I have had a laminectomy,
Way down there, low on the fifth lumbar.
Then, a ruptured disc to add to that.
If you want, I can show you the scar.

I had back pains for ten years or more,
Until my leg was lengthened by prayer.
A retired Episcopal Priest
Asked if I believed in healing prayer.

I said I believed that miracles
Can happen because my faith is there.
Then he said if I truly believed,
I should sit down in the empty chair.

When I did, he knelt in front of me
And took my right foot in his own hand.
I then heard what he prayed, and I know
It was sincere, supplicating, grand.

He prayed that if in His Holy will,
In the will of Jesus up above,
Please lengthen my left leg so all can
See Your pure, powerful healing love.

My leg was lengthened a quarter inch,
Witnessed by many who saw the growth.
We all gave thanks and to Him gave praise.
No more pain from then on. Gospel truth.

Flowers For Caroline

December 9, 2001

God created flowers
For all of us to see.
God created Caroline
And her memories, for me,

The flowers today, red and white;
So bright and full of life,
Are in memory of Caroline,
My Sweetheart and my late Wife.
— from Dick

---

1. Flowers were placed in the sanctuary of Carmel Presbyterian Church as a memorial on the first anniversary of Caroline Davis Turner going to be with Jesus on December 7, 2000.

Hippity Hip

February 16, 2002

I offered my linoleum knife,
Fairly sharp, but not new.
I had a good hacksaw,
The blade was almost new.

My electric power drill
Could drill thick or thin;
Even my rubber hammer
Could drive the new joint in.

Files and sandpaper
To smooth the edges true,
Should prepare those new holes
For my tube of Super-Glue.

I have several big C-clamps
To hold things in place.
It seemed my simple tools
Would give them more space.

My Handy-Dandy sewing kit
Doesn't have any cat-gut;
But I have a real nice stapler
To staple the incision shut.

All of this equipment
I offered free of charge;
Just a little way to help
An operation this large.

The Surgeon thanked me kindly,
But said the tools I offered him
Were just too complicated
To be used to repair a limb.

So he did the operation
And used his own tools.
They must have been pretty good,
Cause my elbow is good as new,
Thank you, Dr. Mason!

In an attempt to help the people of America and the Medicare System in particular, trying to do my part in keeping costs down, and even trying to help the Surgeon save wear and tear on his very expensive equipment, I made the aforementioned offer.

On January 28, 2002, A wonderful surgeon, Dr. J. Bohannon Mason, did a total hip replacement of my left hip. It has been a complete success.

For Diane

Spring 2002

A little sunshine
For a cloudy day,
Returned to you
With our love;
For all you mean,
Past and today,
You've been an Angel
Like from above.

My daughters, Sharyn T. Larson and Nancy T. Blaylock, are sweethearts. And because they are, it is worth it to me to put their actions on paper as a memory.

Sharyn emailed me to ask if I would join her and her sister in expressing their thanks, and mostly love, of their sister-in-love, Diane. She is married to the girls' brother, Rick Tuner.

Diane has been another daughter to me, as she is a sister to the girls. Because Sharyn and Nancy live in the states of Texas and Washington, respectively, they feel Diane has been a representative of the things they would like to do, but can not for obvious reasons.

And it is true. Diane has gone beyond all expectations and desires, at the time of my sweet Caroline's going to be with the Lord, and before that, in 1998, when I almost took the same path. Again, this year when I had a hip replacement, Diane and Rick have been my constant and willing helpers and support.

So, a small way to thank Diane was suggested, by Sharyn and enthusiastically endorsed by Nancy. A way to say "Thank you, sister". And I know they sincerely think of Diane as their sister. At their suggestion, about mid-March, I purchased an Azalea plant, pink and frilly, and delivered it to her home in Ft. Mill, SC. On a card, I wrote the above poem.

Thank you, Diane, and thank you, Sharyn and Nancy, for your caring, attention, and mostly that which makes us all family---LOVE.

Chew On This One

May 4, 2002

Some days are frustrating;
There is not very much fun.
Not much happens, and you
Want to be in the sun.

Some days are so boring,
No excitement at all.
Seems all you do is work.
Won't someone please call?

The housework is all done,
The dishes are all clean.
I need something to do,
Or I just might get mean.

I have been in this house
For many days on end,
No real goal at hand.
I need to call a friend.

But they're all out of town,
At least those I could call;
I bet their days are full,
Active, having a ball!

Not a pity party
Am I having, you see.
I'm just bored, bored to death,
With so much time, so free.

I must find what to do
That will give me some fun.
For days now, it has rained,
Good excuse not to run.

Lacking something to do,
I know this will sound dumb:
I opened a wrapper
And then I chewed some gum.

Son Canyon

June, 2002

Just before Christmas of this past year,
I was given the VBS theme:
Can we do something about canyons?
Start thinking? Seemed like a real bad dream!

But then ideas started to come:
We have that great big Fellowship Hall.
Why can we not make a huge canyon,
Covered with stone on every wall?

Every place kids would go in this place
Needed to remind them about stone.
They needed to explore in the caves,
But never feel that they are alone.

Trying to think like one of the kids,
Wanting to have adventure, but fun,
The caverns and boulders; the caves, too,
Needed to remind kids of the SON.

God made the heavens, and He made earth.
He made rocks, and canyons, and the streams.
He made Carol Harris and programs
That allow our kids to have these dreams.

Of playing in canyons, and loving God.
To learn from our teachers, and to sing,
To play together, and to learn crafts.
And learn love — the most important thing.

So all those listed below these lines
Worked all week to provide Son Canyon.
Some worked days, some several hours.
Some started early, but we had fun.

Some stayed late, some fed the "hired" help.
Some ran errands, some stayed on quite late.
But thanks to all of these faithful folks,
The walls were "stoned" and were first rate!

Thanks to all of you wonderful people who worked long and hard to provide an atmosphere appropriate for the theme for Vacation Bible School at Carmel Presbyterian Church, *Son Canyon*. I love you all!

Advent Story 2002

October 17, 2002 1:40 AM

I had twenty Christmases
Before I met Caroline.
We were newlyweds and love
Made that next Christmas sublime.

It was wartime. Then we found
Our own baby would be due
While I flew airplanes overseas,
But our love would still be true.

Our second Christmas was great!
I flew my missions, and soon
The war ended. I returned
To start life to a new tune.

The years passed, through thick and thin.
The ups and downs of our life
Drew us close, deeper in love.
I had Caroline, my wife.

Now Caroline has passed on,
And how I miss my dear love.
But her Christmas is now spent
With her Sweet Jesus above.

Now is the test I must face:
Will Christmas now be the same?
Of course not! I miss my love!
But to hide would be a shame.

If I try to enjoy this
Happy Season of the year,
I will be honoring the
Joy we shared, year after year.

So this Advent Story is
About the blessings that I
Share in the memories of
Christmas with Caroline. Why?

The blessings from my Dear Lord
Tell me that memories past
Will remind me that the joy
With Caroline will last and last and last.

In Advent Stories of the past, I have looked back and written of long years ago. Now I would like to share what I think those Christmases Past have meant, to let me see what the Lord may have as He leads me into the future.

Boxes, Boxes, Boxes

November 6, 2002

I had already moved to my new house,
And I tried to make it into a home.
Furniture fit into each of the rooms,
And from here I would never, ever roam.

The beds were put into bedrooms with care;
Pots and pans fit nicely on each new shelf.
Towels and washcloths were put in each new bath.
How proud I was of this move by myself!

A nice two-car garage held the surplus
Boxes and tubs of everything I owned.
Dishes, silver, shoes, clothes, soap, and then more.
"But where is my bed comforter?" I moaned!

I moved and shifted more boxes for weeks,
Lifted boxes, unpacked boxes galore.
Where is that comforter? The nights got cool.
I checked and re-stacked those boxes some more.

It took three weeks to solve the mystery.
When one late night, I was inspired to
Go into the garage and realize
There was one box that was just out of view.

It was late at night, but I had to know
What was in that big box, 'neath that big mound?
I heaved and shoved, I pushed, and then I pulled,
But on the bottom, guess what I then found!!!

MY BED COMFORTER!

Thanksgiving 2002

November 29, 2002

It was Thanksgiving Day,
Year two-thousand-two.
Drove thirteen miles to church
With three dozen eggs. True.

My first stop at the church:
The Garden of Love,
The Columbarium,
To pray to God above.

My thoughts of Caroline
Always fill my new day,
And our spirits will join,
As with her I will pray.

Then I joined a fine group,
With my eggs in a sack,
In the warm church kitchen,
Not an egg had a crack.

*The Men's Monday Morning
Prayer Group would all prepare
Breakfast for the whole church,
A gift of love to share.*

*I cracked dozens of eggs,
Even scrambled some, too.
Then I served sausage links.
Only dropped one or two.*

*One of the little boys
Wanted more than his share.
I slipped him extra links.
His parents wouldn't care.*

*Then, when all had been served,
Fellowship in full bloom,
I ate my share, but then,
Still ill, I left the room.*

*Physically, I felt
Worn out and full of cold.
But I wanted to serve
All my friends of old.*

*To the cemetery I drove,
Tho' Caroline's not there.
But I was feeling dour
And needed to share.*

To share my heart of grief,

Overflowing with tears;
To let the wind fly by,
To blow away my fears.

It was as I stood there
In the cold with no sun
That Satan was winning!
I was in depression!

It is real, this illness.
It will destroy my mind.
How will I conquer grief!?
Where's the joy I must find!?

There I stood by that grave,
miserable and cold.
The tears flowed down my face,
Then, I even got bold.

I yelled, "God! Help me, please!"
Out loud, I called for aid!
Lightning did not strike, but
Contact seemed to be made.

I asked for Jesus to
Show me what I must do.
"Please ease the loss of my
Caroline. I need You!"

Then is when I was sure
Depression must not win.

I must live out my life
And try hard not to sin.

Because depression will
Make me sick from within,
If I let it attack,
Then I must bear my sin.

But if I call on You,
My Father up above,
You can cure depression
By sharing Your pure love.

Then I'll be able to
Enjoy my Caroline
Through love-filled memories,
And I will be just fine.

There are times even now,
When grief depresses me.
I just ask for God's love,
And Jesus heals me.

Praise the Lord!
Now I'm fine!

MEMORIES

DECEMBER 7, 2002

It is a tough time of year,
But so is all of the rest.
We all struggle each day, but
This is really not the best.

Anniversaries should be
Celebration from above,
But it is hard not to cry
When you lose someone you love.

But through the tears of each day
Come those memories so grand
Of love, beauty, and fun,
And times when we held her hand.

Two years, but who is counting?
Seventy-seven were made
Into a life to give to us:
Memories of the highest grade.

She used words like "eletrit,"
Phrases that were so funny,
Like cut out or cut ON the light.
Or one about the "burmy."

Each of you kids knows so well
Your special memories, too.
Hang onto them, even cry;
Some to bring a smile or two.

Or share a laugh as you may
Remember her special gift,
A giggle, a hug, a kiss,
To give your spirit a lift.

I send to you on this week
These words of sharing my grief,
Only as a way to help
And bring to me relief.

By sharing our memories
Of your Sweet Mother above,
'Twill help us keep those strong ties
That had to come from our love.

Caroline was my sweet wife,
And Mother to you kids, too.
We all feel this hurtful loss;
Let memories come to you.

Look at them square in the eye,

She is watching from above
To make sure you can smile
At memories of her love.

I love each one of you kids.
Your spouses, I love them, too;
Grandkids, and all those of those Grands,
We'll all make it through.

I do love you.
Daddy, Boo, Boo2,
Dick, Mr. Turner,
Or Hey, you!

---

1. A note to our children two years after Caroline went to be with her Sweet Jesus on December 7, 2000.

Her Guiding Hand

December 17, 2002

I stand here at your gravesite,
My grieving and mourning strong.
When I remember your love,
My heart wants to sing a song.

But words and the melody
Come as tears wrenched from my heart.
Oh, how I miss my true love,
Thinking we would never part.

In heaven, my Caroline
Wants that I may understand:
Serve, and you might hear her voice;
Feel the soft touch of her hand.

Where are you, my Caroline?
Please show me how I can start;
Waiting to hear your sweet voice,
And sense the beat of your heart.

I remember how she loved
To help those who were distressed,
A soft word to ease one's way,
Her helping hand was the best.

I miss you, Caroline love,
Thinking only of my loss,
But you are guiding me home,
Home to Jesus 'neath His cross.

Now I know just where you are,
Guiding me from up above,
To serve others with soft words
And offer a hand, in love.

So I can leave this gravesite,
Smiling cause I understand,
The way to hear your sweet voice,
And we can walk hand in hand.

Who's Counting---I Am

December 25, 2002

If I counted my blessings
By the number of my tears,
They would be like stars above,
Washing away all my fears.

Like the many stars above,
Numbers that are not yet known,
The blessings that come my way
Come from love seeds you have sown.

Because true love is so pure,
Unselfish, giving, and free,
Why you shared and offered it
To me was a mystery.

But you showed me through that love
What it means to give others:
That same love that you gave me,
Crive all sisters and brothers.

So when I did finally
Sow those seeds like I was told,
The mystery was then gone,
Replaced by blessings untold.

I tried, and then I fell short,
But then I tried once again.
And each time I sowed more love,
I would lose more fear and pain.

Those memories bring more tears,
And the tears flow more and more.
Each tear becomes a blessing,
Watering the love you bore.

When you showed that smile of love,
When you gave a helping hand,
It became my own blessing.
A blessing, I understand.

And with the blessing from you,
The memory brings me tears,
Happy tears, number unknown,
That wash away all my fears.

So I will not count the tears,
But count the blessings I get.
Blessings like the stars above---
Counting, but I'm not done yet.

Favorite Words

January 4, 2003

Do you have a favorite word?
Or a word that you like to use?
A word that is seldom spoken,
A word over which you can muse?

For instance, try debilitate.
Or how about reincarnate?
One of my favorite words now
Is a good one: exacerbate.

That is a word for you to use,
A word that makes others wonder
If you really know its use
Or made a terrible blunder.

Use the word indubitable,
And indubitably, you may
Find people who know what you said,
Or they will quickly turn away.

Try the word ineludible,
Then try to "get away with it."
Try the word ineluctable.
I bet you get "away with it."

Do you measure with a quartern,
Or does a quarter ring your bell?
Do you have a favorite word?
Or will the old ones serve you well?

Indubitably, you can have
Fun; exacerbate your speech.
Try out some new words and then pick
Some unsuspecting soul to teach.

I tried this out for a short time,
Until I ran into danger:
I tried to impress and then teach
One who had an English major!

Clouds

January 9, 2003

Have you ever watched the clouds in the sky,
Wondering where they came from, passing by?
Some are so dark, some are gray, some so white.
Heavy dark ones and some feathery light.

As they float through the sky with no support,
Sometimes venting their wrath with a report,
Letting us know they will have their own way,
They will go where they want; we have no say!

When an opening suddenly appears,
The sun peeks through to calm all of our fears,
But the light gets closed out when along comes
Another bully from the big cloud throng.

Some clouds are tall; they go to a great height,
Lumbering along to make such a sight.
Others are small, and the wind speeds them up
Like a kitten or a skittering pup.

Sometimes I think the clouds are very sad,
Either that or they have become very mad,
Because sometimes, even when the sun shines through,
The tears from the clouds can still fan on you.

Clouds come along, from where we do not know.
Sometimes they bring rain and sometimes snow.
They bring shade, lightning, and even some hail,
Fill rivers, refreshing earth without fail.

We see forms with our imagining eyes
As we look up into those cloud-filled skies.
I love to see them as they scoot along,
Almost with the grace of a soothing song.

But the times that the clouds show beauty true
Are when the openings come just for you,
And in the brightness God has let you know
Among the clouds He gave you your rainbow.

Lost In Heaven

January 24, 2003

If we pass the test, and get to heaven,
And get past those Pearly Gates; St. Pete, too,
If the following find eternal life
Up in the clouds where skies are always blue.

Where there is always peace, laughter and joy,
Cooperation, sharing and true love;
Where will I fit in the scheme of those things
That all these people will seek up above?

For those who love to climb a tall mountain,
Or hike trails o'er hills and meadows green,
Will there be a place to sit and day-dream?
And will there be floating clouds to be seen?

There will be those who love the sea and shore.
Who like to watch the great sea billows roar.
There are those who walk beaches by the mile.
And bask in the sun. Will they still get sore?

Some like to fish in streams and in the sea.
Are there fish in heaven, and even rods?
How about those hunters who love the woods.
Guns in heaven? Hunters may be at odds!

I don't speak Greek, nor my English too good.
I may get lost in the woods, or maybe
I might fear the mountain heights, so high up,
And I may not like the sounds of the sea.

Too, others may face the same thing with me:
They may not like those who write silly poems.
Or paint, carve wood, square dance, or some such.
Or times when my imagination roams.

There are so many questions I could ask,
Puzzle over, mull over, and try to
Find an answer for what I need to do
To be able to share these things with you.

Then one day, or maybe it was at night
It dawned on me like a light from above.
It really doesn't matter if there
Are fish, sunburn, or needs for a glove.

We may all dance to a marimba tune,
Or swim in the rolling surf, climb above
The clouds, or roam the forests tall and green.
As long as we know it is all for love.

Because if we are in heaven at all,

It is through knowing and believing in
The Word of our Savior, Jesus the Christ
Who led us there by cleansing us of sin.

So come with me, join in the happy throng,
I won't get lost in heaven because of
Being surrounded with those folks above
Who, like I, got to heaven by Jesus' love.

Boo Who?

February 4, 2003

How many people do you know
Who go around with the name BOO?
Let me tell you of at least three.
This story is really true.

When our first child, a little girl,
Was not yet even a year old,
We started her potty training.
Some may have thought we were too bold.

To start a child so very young,
Especially during the night,
To learn to control this function,
But we thought we were doing it right.

Therefore, periodically,
When we thought the timing was right,
We roused our pretty little girl
To train her. But, oh, what a sight!

She will never remember this,
And perhaps it is just as well.
Because many a time at night,
Off the potty she almost fell.

So to prevent what might have been
A nightly accident or two,
We tried to keep our babe awake
By shaking and calling out "BOO."

She, of course, as all of you, too,
Got through that phase just as did you.
But through the years, reason unknown,
We continued to call her "BOO."

I don't know how one of her friends
Got the same nickname as she, Boo.
But one comes to my mind. Kathy.
She goes through life with that name, too.

Now the third person would be me.
The whole family calls me "BOO."
But I was potty trained for sure
Before I ever got tagged, too.

I was in my fifties at least,
And our house was up on a hill.
I drove a Volkswagen back then.
The sound it made, I can hear still.

Our son, his wife, and their firstborn

*Lived with us temporarily
When his career change came about.
We were a happy family.*

*A little girl was their firstborn,
Pretty and sweet, about age five.
She waited each evening for
That VW to come up the drive.*

*Each right I would open the door,
And then my granddaughter just knew
That the very first thing I would say
When I poked my head in was, "BOO."*

*So she naturally called me "BOO."
She must have thought that was my name.
So for thirty years plus a few,
I answer to BOO without shame.*

*Now you know three people at last,
Three of whom answer when called "BOO."
But to separate my daughter
From me, she now calls me "BOO 2."*

I Just Know

February 11, 2003

I have never seen my Savior's face,
Never even looked into His eyes.
I have never held onto His hand,
Or ever seen His tears when He cries.

I've never seen His footprints in sand,
Or heard a word that He ever said.
Nor have I ever seen Him reach out,
Or even raise someone from the dead.

Never have I seen Him stop and eat,
Or need to take time for a cool drink.
When does He ever have time to read,
To be so smart and know how to think?

It would be nice to hear Him say, "Hi."
Or feel His arms in a great big hug.
Wouldn't it be a lot of pure fun
To have Him give my arm a small tug!

I wonder if He ever just laughs,
Or if He ever wanders around
Like I wander sometimes, all alone,
Content, then sitting on the bare ground.

Do you suppose He knows how to fish,
Bait a hook, chase a squirrel up a tree?
Skate on ice, hit a ball, or play tag
With even a little guy like me?

I guess the answer to all of this
Sounds silly to grown-up folks like you.
Perhaps when I'm older, or wiser,
Then maybe I will feel that way, too.

But I would prefer to have grown folks
Live like little ones, who seem to know
What you grown folks teach us: Jesus loves
Me, I know. The Bible tells me so!

It really doesn't matter much.
All those things I have wondered about.
What really bothers me the most
Is why grown-ups seem to have such doubt.

My life is still simple, you might say,
I will find life changes as I grow.
But until that disillusion comes
Won't you try my way, cause I just know?!!

Restaurant Relief

February 23, 2003

The family decided to go have a treat
By going out for lunch. Give Mom a change Of food.
Paw Paw and Mimi, proud grandparents of their first
Grandson, with his equally proud Mom. What a brood!

So after church, dressed so nice in their Sunday clothes,
They chose their favorite restaurant for their meal.
A nice sit-down meal, with no dishes to wash,
A quiet place to eat, how proud they all would feel.

Show off a sweet, well-mannered baby to all the world.
All smiles, goo-goo talk, a model child was he.
Mommie had nursed him before they went out to eat,
So confidently they ordered, feeling carefree.

Their meals arrived, hot and smelling, oh, so good.
The blessing was said, they felt grateful for this day,
To share this meal together in this restaurant,
In peace and quiet, their cares could all melt away.

No sooner had they started to eat that good food
Than a sudden, rather loud sound beyond belief
Came forth from that sweet, smiling, soft, cuddly babe,
A sound that meant sudden, complete, and true relief.

Well, everyone tried to ignore a sound like that-
Until the air was filled with a second such blast!
That is when Paw Paw decided it required
Action. It required sudden action, but FAST!

Telling the ladies he had things under control,
He scooped up the baby, the diaper bag, and all.
He dashed from the table, where there had been such peace,
And headed for the Men's Room just down the hall.

All seemed quiet in that nice restaurant until
There now came screams from where they had just disappeared.
So up jumps Mama, to the rescue she must go.
Into the Men's Room she flew, the worst she just knew:

Paw Paw must have dropped her baby or, even worse,
Her poor baby boy may have been flushed down the drain!
But what she saw as she opened the Men's Room door
Almost blew her mind, nearly scrambled her poor brain.

Diapers can get loaded, for sure, but this time,
Poor baby overflowed and filled his little shirt.
He filled his pants, but that wasn't the main problem.
Because he was breast-fed, that loud noise was a SQUIRT!

Poor Paw Paw tried to clean his grandson, the best he could,

But by the time Mama got to the messy scene,
It took both of them to wash the crying baby,
And leave the Men's Room clear and then hopefully clean.

Paw Paw loves his grandson, as surely as he should,
But I hope that boy reads this story in belief
That it took a lot of love then, on Paw Paw's part,
The day of his grandson's big restaurant relief.

My Hole-In-One

MARCH 3, 2003

I had an accident, not long ago,
Looking for a cabinet on that day.
'Tweren't my fault they had put that low bed frame
In front of those cabinets, in my way.

But down I went, tore up my leg real bad. But an
angel came by who helped me up
And tried to stop the blood that soaked my "jeans."
Got me a chair as blood seemed to erupt!

Then they called for the Emergency Squad,
Relieving my angel that rescued me.
They wrapped the wound as best as they knew how,
Said a doctor was the one I must see.

What about the golf part?

My angel, Kimberly, had a cell phone,
With which she called my daughter-in-law, who
Called my son at his workplace, so he could

Meet us at an Urgent Care she drove to.

The young doctor took one look at my leg
And said it required more than his skill.
I appreciated his honesty,
So it seemed we needed a hospital.

My son then arrived in the nick of time,
Relieving my angel with thanks profuse,
For coming to my aid, while others stood
Watching; her caring, her van, and its use.

Off to the hospital we did then go,
To the emergency room for more care.
The wound was six inches long down my leg,
And two inches across. A real big tear.

Lots of cleaning, and of course lots of shots,
To deaden the area for what had
To come next: stitches, some inside, some out.
Thirty in all. For those shots, I'm glad.

Where is the golfing part?

So for five weeks I've had my leg propped up,
Changing compresses, wrapping my poor leg
In ace bandages from four to six times
A day. For a change of scenery, I beg!!!

It ended up that the hole was so big,
A few weeks later, they did a skin graft.

It has left a big gap in my right leg.
But a thought came to me. And then I laughed.

Most golfers play with their two healthy legs.
　I did too, but no tournaments I won.
　　If I ever play golf with this poor leg,
　　I can now say I have a hole-in-one.

Dreary Days?

March 30, 2003

Some days seem so dreary,
Rainy, and cloudy, too.
I want to get outdoors.
What's a person to do?

The grass is getting green.
The pond is fuller now.
The trees have some buds, too.
But my head wants to bow.

Ah ha ! ! ! That is my clue,
My head is bowing low.
Is there a signal here?
Something that I should know?

When my head is bowed down,
I have a choice to make:
I can sit and feel sad.
A lonesome path I'll take.

While I am sitting here,
I might, well, even cry.
Feeling like there's no use
For me to even try.

If I am feeling low,
I have another choice.
My challenge to myself:
Listen for my Lord's voice.

How can I hear His voice?
What will I have to do?
I finally found what
You can find. Even you!

All I am asked to do,
To myself, or aloud,
Is say these simple words,
Or are you just too proud?

These simple words have set
So many hearts at ease.
Will you say these words now?
"Help me, Lord. Will you please?"

Now, many days seem dull,
But I can promise you,
If you ask for His help,
Soon you will smile, too.

The rains may stay, 'tis true,

Sunshine is what you need.
But when you ask His help,
At last you've sown the seed

That will chase gloom away.
Now the sunshine will start,
Because you now have your
Lord Jesus in your heart.

When we are lonesome, away from our family and home, needing to get from under the clouds that seem to emotionally have us drained, or have memories of the past joys of life that are not as life is today, we need to have a source of freedom to enjoy a "break in the clouds" that come over us at times. Try this as a way to escape from *Dreary Days*.

Lonesome Salesman

April 13, 2003

Sometimes it is so hard to think,
Because the tears flow from my eyes.
I wonder why I feel so lost.
Year after year after year flies.

Here I sit, thinking of my past,
Thinking I have done pretty good.
I tell no lies, I truly don't;
Hoping I can be understood.

So why am I so sad tonight?
I want to go back to my home,
But I chose to do this type of work,
Knowing that at times I must roam.

If by choice I must leave at times,
Leave those I love the most behind,
Then I must make a choice again
That will give me some peace of mind.

My life is not a pack of lies.
Mistakes are made by all of us.
But that can all be put to rest
With a new life, without a fuss.

It's when we don't know what to do,
And the tears come to flood our soul,
That we need to do just one thing
To reach out for a simple goal.

But if you like those big wet tears,
If you feel like life let you down.
If you are afraid to get well,
Then go ahead — those tears will drown

Even a big man grown like you.
But if you are willing to try
To find peace, even when alone,
Don't let this challenge pass you by.

First, you must accept where you are.
Stop feeling sorry for yourself.
Realize you are a man now.
Not a puppet up on a shelf.

You can use all of this spare time
To strengthen your body and mind.
You can be all you want to be,
But you must be willing to find

The strength that put you where you are

And ask for that strength to help you
Seek and believe what you now need:
Faith in the Word, honest and true.

All by yourself, get on your knees.
Or sit in a chair, lie on the bed.
Position is unimportant.
It's your heart that needs to be fed.

It is so simple, please trust me.
Just ask Jesus to be your friend.
Tell him you are lonesome tonight,
And your heartache you want to end.

Pick up the bible and open
It to the Book of John, to start.
Read what it says, gain strength, and then
Ask Jesus to speak to your heart.

If you will try, really try,
Be faithful to what you have read,
Live what you learn, don't be ashamed,
Your body and mind will be fed.

Times will come when you'll feel alone.
Remember, you made that choice when
You asked Jesus into your heart.
You'll never be lonesome again.

Reunion

April 21, 2003

Who am I to weep and cry,
Even if there are clouds in the sky?
Soon the clouds will pass me by,
Knowing you are with Jesus on high.

Just put flowers on your grave,
But it is my soul for Him to save.
So I must not rant and rave.
Memories of you will keep me brave.

Memories of your smile sweet,
Your total being from head to feet.
Life will someday be complete
When again in heaven we will meet.

I believe Jesus was raised.
My life changed, so I am not amazed
That someday I will be raised.
Then, hand in hand, His name will be praised.

In some form we'll meet up there,
But in that heavenly place is where
We'll be a fortunate pair,
United with Him up in the air.

In a place with no more tears.
No hurry nor rush, and no more fears.
No waiting 'til the storm clears.
Just serving Jesus because He hears

Laughter, singing all the time.
And in that heavenly place, no crime.
To be sure this ends in rhyme,
We will all bask in His love sublime.

Retirement!!?

May 17, 2003

Sharyn was a sweet little babe,
The first of our three great children.
It seems like yesterday to me
That she was so very small. THEN!

Look at her now, a woman grown,
With a flock of grandkids to love.
How did the years fly by so fast?
Did someone give those years a shove?

Remember those first grades of school?
The times we went to the beach?
The scar on your arm from the time
You chased a ball you could not reach?

Our years in sunny Florida
Were fun during your high school years.
Thinking you were in love, your prom,
So much laughter, and a few tears.

But you survived those trials of life,
As we got through those hurricanes.
Then it was time to leave your home
For F S U to stretch your brains.

You had fun and studied some, too.
Got your degree, but wanted more.
Earned your Master's Degree, lil gal,
Your parents could ask for no more.

You went in search of your own life,
A family someday, a home,
An opportunity to serve,
And find your man. No more to roam.

All this happened in such short time,
And so far away! In Plano! Plano?
Plano? Of course. Texas? Oh, no!
So far away! So far to go!

Of course, there was a man for you,
The man of your life named Jerry.
A tall Texan, just meant for you.
The man you said you would marry.

So you did. Then guess what happened:
Soon two little ones of your own
That would grow as fast in your life,
As fast as to us you had grown.

The years have flown. Your family grew.

RETIREMENT!!?

I know not where all those years went.
But suddenly you send me word:
YOU now plan on RETIREMENT!!!

My little girl, just starting school,
Is ready for RETIREMENT!
How can this be? It makes me feel
As old as the Old Testament!

Your mother has gone with the Lord,
Happy up in heaven on high.
Such pride and joy she must feel for
You, must surely cause her to cry.

But soon her tears will go away,
Cause Sharyn's years have been well spent,
Sharing and caring for others,
As she will in RETIREMENT ! ! !

I will try to live with this odd
Feeling that time has slipped by me.
That it went too fast, or I missed
What it was meant for me to see.

It has been a good life, even
If it has been a sort of whirl.
Sharyn may take retirement, but
She will always be my little girl.

Oh, Bearded One

June 8, 2003

There once was a man who grew a beard, To
be in character for a part
In an Easter program. So he thought
It was time to stop shaving. A start!

At first, he could not go in public
Because he had injured his right shin.
He had to keep it elevated,
So for several weeks he stayed in.

Talk about getting cabin fever!!!
One thing he could do as a shut-in
Besides sit, read, and watch the TV:
Let hair grow on his chinny-chin-chin.

So the fuzz grew and turned to stubble.
It was not a very pretty sight.
But it was for a noble, good cause.
He needed the beard to look just right.

The time approached for the Easter show.
The whiskers grew at a slow, slow pace.
His part was of High Priest Caiaphas.
He needed those whiskers on his face!!!

His leg had improved so he could stand.
His beard finally was a goatee.
He played his part as Caiaphas and
Displayed his beard for the world to see.

The beard was to be shaved the next day,
But the ladies said it looked sexy,
Dapper, smart, good looking, and some said
It just fit, made me look more like me.

Days went by, then weeks of no shaving,
Made that goatee fill out. Holy Cow!
Even have to trim that part of me,
And I have gotten used to it now!!

I grew the beard to play Caiaphas,
And some joke and call me by that name.
But now my goatee has played a trick,
And the reference is not the same.

I still have the goatee, trim and neat.
But nature now gives me a reason
To let this fuzzy, hairy beard grow:
I call it my beard for each season.

We have had so much rain this spring.

The streams and rivers now overflow.
People now ask this bearded one if
I am Noah, building my ark to go?

Ring

June 24, 2003

The telephone rang today.
Caught it on the second ring.
With delight it was to
Hear Julie. She seemed to sing.

There was a lilt in her voice,
Though she's always full of fun.
But I had an idea.
This call meant the deed was done.

The deed, of course, was the news
That made her smile, and heart glad,
Eric had proposed last night---
Gave her all the love he had.

She called me, to my delight,
She knew I wanted to share
In my granddaughter's true love
In her life, because I care.

But what was special to me
And caused my old heart to sing:
The diamond that Eric
Used was from Caroline's ring.

Caroline, my wife, now gone
To heaven with her Sweet Lord,
Was Julie's grandmother who
Loved Julie, whom she adored.

On September twenty-nine,
Nineteen forty-four, you see,
That diamond was given
To my Caroline, from me.

Now it will always be worn
On the third finger, left hand,
Of granddaughter Julie on
Her own engagement ring band.

This causes me a few tears;
Sentiment, emotions, love,
Because I know in my heart,
This all came from God above.

Four-Letter Words

July 18, 2003

Everyone knows my Caroline
Was the very love of my life.
I was the luckiest guy to
Have her for my sweet, loving wife.

She never used the Lord's dear name
In vain or swore. But honestly,
It will shock you when you can see
Her four-letter words used on me!

I list these words, for you to see
How Caroline would seem to find
Words that got my attention when
Some sort of housework got behind.

I knew she was about to use
A four-letter word when she spoke,
"Richard!" (Otherwise it was "Dick.")
I knew then this would be no joke.

So here are those four-letter words
That I came to really know
When Caroline would mean business
And attention I must bestow:
Work, Wipe, Yard, Wash
Toil, Walk, Bush, Fall
Trim, Hose, Rake, Fill
Leaf, Read, Blow
Rest, Vac'm, Sitt

There are more, but at this moment,
Just thinking about what all of
These words meant: so much work! Oh, well,
I know she said those words with love.

We used to laugh at all those words.
We teased. We joked. We loved. But then,
How I miss those four-letter words.
Caroline has gone to heaven.

Turtles & Rabbits

JULY 23, 2003

I have prostate cancer,
But don't fret over me.
I have a few more days,
Even years, hopefully.

I tell you this, my friend,
Not to get sympathy.
I have got a story
To tell, so stay with me.

I honestly feel great.
My calendar is full,
I do what I durn please,
My own weight I can pull.

So don't feel sorry, please.
Maybe the tests are wrong.
Somehow I feel they're right,
But I feel healthy. Strong.

This is the story. How
They explained it to me:
They discovered the cells
In my prostate, you see.

They were hot, aggressive,
Eight on a scale of ten.
Some were slow: the turtles.
Some were like rabbits, then.

My treatment by hormones
Killed those cells, the turtles.
But that was just one of
The cancer cell hurdles.

There still remained those cells,
Those represented by
The rabbits that escaped.
Some were quick, fast, and sly.

After a couple years,
Those tricky, fast rabbits
Showed what rabbits can do:
Multiply. There's no quits!

Soon, we found in my tests:
My PSA went sky high.
My bone scan was ok.
We wondered why, oh, why.

Those tricky little cells,

Labeled rabbits by some,
Were hiding some place else.
Where were they, and how come?

So they put an implant
In my arm to give me
A daily dose of drug
To kill rabbits, you see.

But still there are rabbits
Hiding some place, somewhere.
Cancer cells, they tell me,
Running loose in me. WHERE!?

They kill lots of rabbits.
But I think now I know
The reason rabbits die
Is obvious: Oh, WOE!

I'm PREGNANT!!

My Dear Friend Arthur Lynip

August 18, 2003

How the years have passed by.
World War I was not
Even about to start.
The Archduke was not shot!

Well, at least not shot yet!
But I bet you recall
When Armistice Day came,
And hopes of peace for all.

For a while, remember
Those gay twenties, back when
Flappers danced, bootleggers
Boozed like there was no sin.

The stock market went bust.
But good things happened, too.
Linberg, all by himself,

Flew o'er the ocean blue.

FDR with three terms,
Social Security,
The WPA Act, and WWII.
Now we're free?

Education now thrived, and
Atom bombs were a threat.
Jets broke the speed of sound.
You ain't seen nothin' yet.

Man built tall buildings and
Even walked on the moon.
Man seems to be so smart.
He may go to Mars soon.

In spite of all those things,
Man has not found what's true.
That is- don't be ashamed
To say, "I do love you."

Arthur, because of you,
We in this class have known
Someone who is for us.
A role model and grown

To know someone who has
Lived through all the above,
Given of yourself, too.
Someone we can all love.

Yes, the years have passed by.
But one thing stays the same:
We know God has shown us A
friend. Arthur's his name.

My dear friend Arthur Lyrip: What an occasion for us members of the Knowing His Word Sunday School Class to come together and honor our esteemed friend. Ninety years carries so many memories. I am only eighty next March, so you have become a role model for me.

What Is This Christmas Thing?

SEPTEMBER 23, 2003

What's going on? What's all that noise?
Sleigh bells ring. Are you listening?
Where did you get all those toys?
The snow in tree tops glistening!

How can you afford all that?
This happens just once a year.
Those lights might burn your house down!
No. We have nothing to fear.

Everyone is so happy.
You could be that happy, too.
Bah! Humbug! I'll keep what's mine.
Sharing is what you should do.

Why should I share? What's the point?
Gifts from the heart will bring love.
Why should I give? Tell me why.

The best gift came from above.

You mean Santa in his sleigh?
Christmas celebrates Christ's birth.
Then it's not this Santa thing?
We praise God for all we're worth.

But all this tinsel and noise?
We sing carols and give.
Should I listen to the words?
Give gifts from the heart and live.

But I don't know any friend.
Give freely and make a friend.
Maybe someone from a church?
It matters not how much you spend.

But should I give, just to give?
Give from your heart to give joy.
Will this help me understand?
Go buy some food and a toy.

If I do that, will it help?
Go share the toy and the food.
Must I join in all that noise?
You can, will, do something good.

So that is what I must do?
Come join in this happy throng.
So it is joy, not all noise?
You've missed such joy, these years long.

> ***Yes, I will do as you say.***
> *Share, give, sing. It's time to start.*
> ***The noise is gone, and lights shine bright.***
> *Jesus is now in your heart.*
>
> ***The gift I'll give is for joy.***
> *Christmas carols you now sing.*
> ***I'll freely, joyfully give.***
> *Now enjoy **This Christmas Thing!***

For someone who never liked poetry as a student, or even as an adult, it surprises me when the Lord tells me to go write certain words or lines. The problem with this is that I really have to stretch my mind and vocabulary. It is a challenge to get words to not only rhyme, but also keep the meter right.

That is what happened today, when I came across the reminder about the Advent Book for this year. It was due in October, but the Lord seemed to suggest the following theme and dialogue. Christmas? After reviewing the past contributions I had made in some past Advent Books, I figured maybe next year. The Lord has His own timetable. Was He telling me I may not be able to write next year? (I hope not!) Or was He telling me to obey Him?

As a result, the verses that follow are an admonition to me to keep Christmas in the proper perspective and to remember: *What Is This Christmas Thing?*

Three Brothers

September 27, 2003

Once there were three brothers.
There are three brothers, still.
One was the eldest one.
That must be a big thrill.

Of course, one was the youngest.
That seems to make good sense.
He will remain the youngest
Now and from this day hence.

And then in the middle,
One more brother is there.
Not to be the elder,
Nor the youngest by far.

Much was expected from
The firstborn, of course, and
The youngest would be the
Baby, cute and so grand.

What to do with the one
who was not last or first?
He just fits in between,
Not to be best or worst.

So if you are the first,
Enjoy your position.
And if you are the last,
Enjoy the attention.

If by chance you're the one
In the middle, OK.
Cause you can be happy,
And stay out of the way.

When all of life is done,
And everything is said,
It won't matter at all,
Cause we will all be dead.

Our Commitment

October 4, 2003

While I was out playing this game,
Which is better known as soccer,
Little did I know that one day
It would lead me to the altar.

Do let me explain what I mean.
Soccer is a game played for fun.
It is a form of exercise
Because you have to run---and run.

But it has other benefits,
Because it takes several to play.
For a long time, I played for fun.
Especially this certain day.

Among the group who played that day
Was this new fellow who was quick
To fit in with the rest of us.
He told us his name was Eric.

Over a period of time,
This friendship did not seem to yield.
In fact, we soon became good friends,
Both on and off the soccer field.

Well, things progressed along quite well.
Dating soon became a sure thing.
Soccer became more than a game.
Seeing Eric made my heart sing.

But time went on as we became
More than friends. It seemed more like love.
But time went on. More soccer, too.
Did he need a sign from above?

I guess it did. My birthday night,
Eric said we would celebrate.
Little did I know he had plans
Just for me on this special night.

Roses were there on the table.
We ordered our food. What a treat.
But something was not going right.
Eric was nervous, did not eat.

Would he ask me tonight if I'd
Be Mrs. Eric McCartney?
Was this only a birthday date?
I would just have to wait to see.

After all, the card only read

OUR COMMITMENT

"Happy Birthday, love, Eric" — so
My hopes were not met this night. (But
What happened next set me aglow!)

It was just a birthday dinner
After all. Then he suggested
I order dessert. So I did.
But he had made some plans ahead.

The waiter brought a tray on which
Was a small box, 'neath a napkin.
That is when my tears overflowed,
And my heart seemed to leap within.

On bended knee, my Eric asked
If I would become his dear wife.
Of course, my answer was "Oh, yes."
I would be the rest of my life!

Oh, how the tears started to flow,
Cause now I could say with no shame,
You never can really tell
The results from a soccer game.

You, too, may someday fall in love,
Playing a game like soccer, too.
But I bet you won't get a poem
Written by my granddad named Boo.

This is for my special granddaughter Julie Larson on her marriage to Eric McCartney, October 4, 2003, with love always. Remember your commitment.

Butterfly Angels

October 24, 2003

Once, so many years ago,
My Caroline fell in love
With beautiful butterflies
That she saw come from above.

Actually, they seemed to
Swarm about, out of the blue.
It seemed like they were a cloud,
Undulating as they flew.

They were Monarch butterflies,
Migrating as Monarchs do.
They mesmerized Caroline
Until they were out of view.

Then she heard that butterflies
Were the symbol of rebirth.
And to us Christians, rebirth
Means life after life on earth.

*My beautiful Caroline
Wore a butterfly pin when
She went out. This she did 'til
She met Jesus in heaven.*

*Then our granddaughter Julie
Met Eric as time went by.
Julie is called "Butterfly"
By Eric. I asked him why.*

*Once he held a butterfly
In his hand, and someone said,
"If you love this, set it free.
It may come to you instead.*

*"To be yours forevermore.
If it you no longer see,
It no longer comes back,
You'll know it was not to be."*

*Julie went away to school.
Eric then went on his way.
The "butterfly" he had met
Seemed to have just flown away.*

*Seven years have now gone by.
Julie came back home at last.
Back to Eric's life again.
There was that phrase from the past.*

Had the butterfly returned?

He thought he had set her free.
But she had returned again.
Surely this was meant to be.

Time went on, as time will.
Love blossomed, as love will.
Eric and Julie are wed
To love until time stands still.

So butterflies that return
Mean love, and a life rebirth.
Could it mean a butterfly
Is an angel here on earth?

You see, my Caroline is
In heaven. But could it be
She wanted to let us know
She returned, for us to see

That her love is eternal,
Like a returning butterfly?
In fact, we are very sure,
And I will now tell you why.

As the mother of the bride,
Our daughter, Sharyn Larson,
Stepped out of her home on the
Morn after the occasion,

To meet with all the wedding
Party for a fond farewell.

She knew that her mother had
Been with all of us as well.

Because as she left to go,
A Monarch butterfly flew
Right there in front of her face,
Then away into the blue.

Julie returned to Eric.
To be his forevermore.
My Caroline returned, too.
I love her forevermore.

The UTI Blues

November 25, 2003

I can not resist writing this.
It may get your quick attention.
Just the name tells you it's no fun:
Urinary Track Infection.

Mostly women get this problem,
But it can sometimes hit men, too.
No need to explain the reasons.
Different anatomy will do.

But when it hits the male sex,
Well, at least so I have been told,
Treating it is much more profound,
Especially if the male is old.

Well, I fit all of the above.
I am male, and I can prove it.
And this infection that I had
Sure did give me a hissy-fit!

I will not go into symptoms.
If you don't know, then ask a friend.
But I tell you, it is no fun.
Nature calls like there is no end.

The Doc said I had a UTI.
An infection that's hard to treat.
But he said he knew what to do,
And my infection he would beat.

Heavy doses by injection
Of a drug that should do the trick.
After two weeks of getting shots,
I should be well, no longer sick.

The doses were of such a strength.
Still, it took two syringes each time.
Every other day for two weeks,
It made me think, "The walls I'll climb!"

The nurse told me to drop my pants,
Take a deep breath, and relax.
Taking a deep breath was easy.
The hard part was dropping my slacks.

The first shot was done very well.
The next one in the other bun
Was no problem, so the first day
Of treatment was over and done.

Every other day, I came back.

Each time, it was more of the same.
But after about the fourth time,
I was getting tired of this game.

I had four more shots yet to get,
But eight shots in the buns had me
A little bit tender and sore,
Wanting to get well and be free.

When at last I finished all twelve
Of those shots in my tender rear,
I realized the UTI
Was something for us all to fear.

The infection is bad enough.
That alone can cause you to fear.
But the treatment seemed so much worse:
Twelve heavy shots in my poor rear!!!

I thank the doctor for his cure.
The poor nurse, I felt sorry for.
But it was my butt that got shot,
And, in the end, sure did get sore.

Pun intended!

CAROLINES GIFT

JANUARY 21, 2004

All through the fifty-six years and two months
That Caroline lived as my loving wife,
We laughed a lot, and we sure gave a lot.
But her best gift was her gift of her life.

I miss her. Sure, I miss my Caroline.
We lived as close as two peas in a pod.
We lived and loved, we talked and even shared
Our faith and trust in our eternal God.

Caroline seemed to lead the way for me,
By being able to express her love
For her "Sweet Jesus" that she knew so well.
She was always aware of Him above.

Sure, I believed there was a God up there;
I knew the story of Jesus' life.
But somehow, all of this spiritual
Faith was not like that of my dear sweet wife.

Over the years, my faith finally grew.
I came to know and trust more in my Lord.
But I never learned to be completely
Dependent on His guidance and Holy Word.

But Caroline had led me the right way,
Showed me by her loving and steady life
How I could lead my life serving my Lord,
And be able to handle times of strife.

Strife came indeed when I lost Caroline.
Fifty-six years and two months of love
Left me as half of what I used to be
When her "Sweet Jesus" took her up above.

But I now know what a beautiful gift
Caroline gave me at her final breath.
She was at rest and at peace, this I know.
She gave me a smile and overcame death.

It was then that I knew without a doubt
That her smile was assurance, just for me.
What she had told me through all of those years
Was now reality for me to see.

Caroline's passing will always be for
Me sad, but a sweet spiritual lift
In my faith, trust, and love of my dear Lord.
There's nothing greater than Caroline's gift.

My Son

March 14, 2004

It was rather late in the night
When Caroline said, "We must go!"
We had gone to bed. I had slept.
But her anxious voice let me know

Her labor pains were earnest now.
She was sure. Not just "wait and see!"
Our second child was on its way.
A girl for her? A boy for me?

Our first child was a girl, so sweet.
Would our second child be a boy?
Would we have hand-me-downs for her,
Or would a truck be a better toy?

Back in nineteen forty-seven,
Ultra-sound was not even known.
You waited till the babe was born
To see how the "plumbing" had grown.

My mother-in-law was a nurse
And was concerned, naturally.
So she went to the hospital
With Caroline, baby, and me.

Well, the hours dragged on slowly.
Our senses seemed to grow faint.
But Mom and I drank hot coffee,
Strong enough to use to thin paint.

At last, we were told Caroline
Delivered a bundle of joy:
We already had our sweet girl,
And now a bouncing baby boy.

What joy it was to see him grow,
And build toys for him to enjoy.
Carriage parts here, roller skates too.
Then playing catch with my own boy.

There were toy guns, allowed back then.
He joined the Cubs and Boy Scouts, too.
He played Little League ball. Good, too.
Got in a scrap or two. Boys do.

He grew up tall. Good looking, too.
Graduated High School, of course.
Had fun with girls, being that age.
Then he joined the U. S. Air Force.

Got out of the Armed Services,

Then he got his college degree.
Of course, marriage and children, four.
Served in his church and was happy.

There is beauty in all of this.
His Mom in heaven smiles down,
Knowing that she raised a good man,
And some day he would have his crown.

But I want to give him his crown
While I can still thank him, you see,
For what he did the other day
Before I had my surgery.

He asked to pray right at that time,
For all involved, and when they're done,
To get me well. But I was healed
By that prayer offered by my son.

In calm voice, his words all came through.
The words flowed from God up above.
I thank my son for his good life
And his soft prayer so full of love.

Seeking Sincerity

JUNE 10, 2004

*I finally think that I may
Have gotten closer to my God,
Because my thoughts are now of Him,
Thanking Him through each day I trod.*

*But as hard as I try each day
To practice His presence in me,
I know that if I have to try,
I must lack true sincerity.*

*Perhaps I am getting better
In my sincerity at last,
Because I find that I do not
See people as in the years past.*

*So in my humble, stumble way,
I look for good as best I can.
And tho' I failed in years gone by,
I've learned to love my fellow man.*

But still I want to know my God,
To thank Him and really show
That, insincere as I may be,
In His true love I want to grow.

I don't know what my God looks like,
I don't know His age or His size.
I can only imagine Him
As Almighty, completely wise.

It matters not to me at all
Where He lives way up above.
Or if He is thin, short, fat, or tall,
As long as He shows me His love.

Just let me be in his presence.
Let me go where the Saints now trod,
So He can wipe tears from my eyes,
And I can touch the face of God.

OH, COUNTRY 'TIS OF THEE---RING

JUNE 23-27, 2003

'Twas a long time ago,
'Fore Christmas, I recall.
That 'li'l farmer daughter---
call'd carol to all y'all,

Said Vacation Bible
School theme fer this here yeer
Was farm stuff fer th' kids
Like chickin, hogs 'n steer.

I wuz askt fer my thauts,
So I set down to think.
No fain is quite complete
'Thout a barn 'n hay steer.

So I told her I'd build
A 'li'l barn fer her farm.
But she wanted even more:

Bild her a cuntry store!!!

So I mezured an' drew.
Drew an' mezured some more.
When I at last got dun,
I had th' barn an' store.

Thet wuz th' eezy part.
Someone had to bild these
Bildins fer VBS!!!
Craftsmen don't grow on trees.

I rekrutid some men.
Had a meetin' won mite.
Giv'd them copies of plans.
They all sed, "All right!!!"

David Rudd got fer us,
Carbored fer all th' walls.
He even brung 'nuf stuff
To bild a few cow stalls.

Bob Scull and Al Purtill
Pre-cut lumber to size.
Th' nex' morn we cood not
Beleev wif our our eyes

Wat they did done; but then,
Wif thet big start, nex day
Harold Blackmon, Roy Rowe,
They shun did em there pay,

OH, COUNTRY 'TIS OF THEE---RING

David Cariaga
Was No. 1 "goffer."
Thet meens he wuz almost,
But not quite, a loafer.

He carried timbers and
Fetched tools fer all thos who
Put peeses of thet wood
Together - tried an' true.

Bob Mllis is so tall,
No ladder did he need.
He lifted an' nailed,
Swift as you ever see'd.

Curt Rogers had in tow
Taylor, son of Roy Rowe.
They, with Roy (what a team!),
Made th' Country Store grow.

Marvin Clifford wuz there
To hep build all those shelves.
Holly and Grant Chambers
Wurk't on barn trim like elves.

Laurel Thompson shur draw'd
Those lines to look like wood.
All roun' th' store, an' then
Made th' barn trim look good.

FROM BOO, WITH LOVE

This story could niver
Be dun wifout labers
From one more who done helped.
Her name is Beth Chambers.

All thos abuv done good.
They all worked very hard.
But Beth clim'd ladders, too.
But not in th' ban yard.

All th' guys wen they arrived
Wore shorts when they came in.
What I am 'bout to say,
You may think is a sin.

Werk fer werk, all werkt hard.
But this much I recall:
Beth wuz best lookin', wif
Best lookin' legs of all.

Al an' Bob, Dave an' Grant'
Holly, David, an' Curt,
Marvin, Laurel, Harold,
Jus' think no 'un got hurt.

Roy an' his son Taylor,
Bob an' Beth, God bless y'all.
You'us done reel good
When you anserd th' call.

But th' ban got put up,

An' th' Country Store, too.
When you see thos' abuv
Hug them an' say "THANK YOU!"

A tribute to all those who constructed the farm-theme sets for Vacation Bible School for June 23 - 27, 2003, *Son Harvest*.

What Is That Trophy

There is a trophy in my study.
There is no other just like this one.
It consists of some wood, a Clorox cap,
And a small piece of gray granite stone.

But what makes the trophy so unique
Is the .22 caliber shell.
It is empty, having been fired.
That is the story that I must tell.

To make the story a mystery,
And to add intrigue just for the fun,
There is a hole in the bottle cap.
But there is no sign of any gun.

My wife Caroline and I went to
Visit my cousin and his wife, too,
Who lived at the foothills in Vestal, New
York. Oh, what a beautiful view.

They had built a hunting cabin way
Out in the Catskill wild rolling hills.
A place where you could be all alone,
Where you could leave all your woes and ills.

They hunted deer and wild turkeys,
Sometimes with arrows and trusty bow.
They lived free from smog and noisy towns,
In spring, summer, fall, and winter snow.

Cousin Dick was a pretty good shot;
I thought that I was pretty good, too.
So we decided to shoot targets.
Away from camp, in the woods, that's true.

Cousin Bev was busy, so she told
Caroline to go along with us.
Caroline never shot a gun much,
But then she didn't put up much fuss.

Well, into the woods we three did go,
To do this great sharpshooting event.
I hoped to show my trusting, sweet wife
She married a real gun-totin' gent.

This sharpshooting trio plinked away
At tree stumps, cans we had brought along.
Even Caroline showed she could shoot.
To her, target practice was not wrong.

We soon decided we were ready

To show Caroline how we could shoot,
With superior concentration,
Determination, and skill to boot.

An empty plastic Clorox bottle
Would be our final target that day.
So each loaded the rifle in turn,
And we made a plastic sieve that way.

Well, Caroline did her share, so we
Figured we needed to show her how
To separate the men from the---gal,
A true test must be made here, right now.

The Clorox bottle had a small cap.
No bigger than a nickel in size.
Dick and I, confident at long last,
Would now take home the bottle cap prize.

Thirty paces, propped up on a stump,
We placed that tiny cap colored blue.
A single shot was put in the gun,
And then Dick aimed, so sure and so true.

Surely the cap must have moved a bit
Because Dick's shot missed by a thin hair.
How could he miss so simple a shot
When he had aimed with such skill and care?

Well, at least I would show Caroline
How the shot was to be done this day.

So I loaded a shell in the gun,
Stood tall, aimed, and I fired away.

Of course, the bullet went straight and true.
Right on target! Or so I had thought
I had hit that bottle cap for sure.
But it was as pristine as when bought!

The shot must have been more difficult
Than anticipated it to be.
But we would give Caroline a chance
To try a shot. Good sports we would be.

So then Caroline picked up the gun,
Chambered a shell, confident and sure.
She put the stock to her shoulder. Then,
Aimed at the target without demur.

She pulled the trigger. We heard the sound.
She had taken us up on the dare.
She watched with us as that projectile
Left the gun and flew through the cool air.

Well, after I saw the hole in that
Clorox cap, and heard that gun go "BAM,"
I knew from then on when Caroline
Called, I would salute and say "YES, MA'AM!"

I picked up that spent twenty-two shell,
A piece of local stone, and the best

Part of the whole event, and carried
That "holy" cap home---you know the rest.

Berod At Times

912:2LRJR'

When you run out of things
To write about sometimes,
It becomes a challenge
To mix up words or lines.

So use the fsrit lteetr
Of ecah wrod for a sratt,
The lsat lteetr cmeos lsat.
Now flil the mdilde prat

With all the ltesetr lfet,
Lkcisadciaslaly.
Wow! What a way to slepl!
This wlil dvire fklos czray!

Sreuly trehe are bieetr
Wyas to fhgit tihs brodrroe.
But this took some rael fuhgoht.
Csae you tnihk I am dmub.

But if you want to divre
Fklos way up a iere,
Thry witning this sane poem
Bkorcadws. But dno.t clal me!!1

---

1. Second stanza (So use the first letter, Of each word for a start, The last letter comes last, Now fill the middle part)

About

RICHARD W. TURNER, SR.

RICHARD W. TURNER, SR. (1924-2004) was a World War II veteran, decorated pilot, artist, author, and devoted husband and father whose life was marked by service, creativity, humility, and deep faith.

First Lt. Dick Turner, 1944

Born in Johnson City, New York, Turner answered the call of duty, serving with distinction in the China-Burma-India (CBI) Theater. As a pilot, he flew 72 1/2 missions over the treacherous Himalayan supply route known as "The Hump", an experience that shaped his character and perspective for the rest of his life.

Richard W. Turner, Sr.

After the war, Turner became a leader in the Boy Scouts of America, raised a family, was active in his church, and enjoyed painting, nature, and whittling woodcarvings. He shared 56 years with the love of his life, Caroline, and began writing in his later years to reflect on his life's most defining moments.

Also by

Richard W. Turner, Sr.

Third Chance, 2nd Edition

Third Chance
An inspiring memoir chronicling a near-death experience and spiritual awakenings. With heartfelt gratitude, he shares the faith, friendships, and miracles that shaped his life and restored his purpose. This memoir honors the love of his life, Caroline, and the encouragement and support of his family and community.

Revelation ---at last, 2nd Edition

Revelation ---at last

A heartfelt journey through love, loss, and eternal hope. In this intimate work, Turner reflects on the life he shared with his beloved wife Caroline and the emotional and spiritual path he walked since her passing. Through personal stories and scriptural reflections, he offers comfort and clarity on the promise of eternal life and reunion with those we love in Christ.

Stories from the Hump, 3rd Edition

Stories from The Hump

A vivid and moving collection of war time memories. The stories from Turner's service as a US Army Air Corps C-46 pilot flying over the Himalayas blend danger, humor, and the unseen hand of God. Turner captures the courage and faith of those brave airmen who flew The Hump in the China-Burma-India Theater of WWII.

www.ingramcontent.com/pod-product-compliance
Lightning Source LLC
Chambersburg PA
CBHW070328010526
44107CB00004B/454